Disciple the Nations!

By Peace not Pressure

Edward N. Gross

Foreword by Pastor Saqib Munawar

Parson's Porch Books

Disciple the Nations!
ISBN: Softcover 978-1-960326-17-1
Copyright © 2023 by Edward N. Gross

All Scripture quotations, unless otherwise indicated, are taken from the English Standard Version of the Bible copyright 2001 by Crossway, a publishing ministry of Good News Publishers.

Parson's Porch Books is an imprint of Parson's Porch *&* Company (PP*&*C) in Cleveland, Tennessee. PP*&*C is a self-funded charity which earns money by publishing books of noted authors, representing all genres. Its face and voice is **David Russell Tullock** (dtullock@parsonsporch.com).

Parson's Porch *&* Company *turns books into bread & milk* by sharing its profits with the poor.

www.parsonsporch.com

Disciple the Nations!

Dedication

I lovingly dedicate this book on how to fulfill the Great
Commission of Jesus,
the Prince of Peace, by peace not pressure, to four peacemaking
servants of God:

My parents
Dr. Ralph and Ruth Gross (medical missionaries to Africa), and
Debby's parents
Dr. Robert and Ruth Dickerson (long-time pastoral servants to
America)

Contents

Foreword

How rare is this book? In the 75-year history of the Islamic Republic of Pakistan, and during my 16 years of ministry in my beloved Pakistan, and in Afghanistan and UAE, I have never read the phrase, "evangelism through peace not by pressure." Being a 5th generation Christian, and having observed many Christian apologists and scholars trying to defend Christianity, I simply ask, how much good has that approach done? As recent as March 2023, I read a challenge on social media by a Christian debater, who is willing to defend Jesus Christ and Christianity by answering any Islamic scholar's challenge of the deity of Christ. Frankly, in my opinion, we are just wasting our time with this approach. We are winning few souls this way, and, in fact, are creating an environment of hatred though we are called to be the children of love.

What has so dramatically changed my perspective about the future of Christianity in Pakistan? Dr. Edward N. Gross' book, *Are you a Christian or a Disciple?*, came into my hands and, when I read the title, I thought it would be worthwhile to read. Well, I ended up reading it three times, and becoming convinced that this focus on following Jesus as disciples with peace is the dire need of Pakistan today. Its message will help produce a paradigm shift here, as we were on the wrong path of debating, defending and evangelizing with pressure. And due to this, lots of people have lost their lives by severe persecutions and hatred.

I requested and was accepted by Dr. Gross to let us translate and print this book into our Urdu Language. He did not just accept our request, but also helped find funding for the whole project. Then I thought it would be more fruitful if he could come in person and introduce the subject to our nation's ordained and youth leadership. What was the result of his coming to Pakistan and teaching different denominational leaders, seminary students, theologians, and Bishop Councils? They all were shocked as they listened to his teachings. It was an eye-opening moment for all of us. We discovered that we were making church members not disciples. We were doing evangelism with pressure not with peace. Now, the majority of our national leaders have agreed and become committed to using the biblical approach of "evangelism by peace not by pressure" going forward.

Some Bible Colleges and Seminaries embraced Dr. Gross' challenging teaching and agreed to make it a regular part of their Curriculum. They will use the main book, "Are you A Christian or A Disciple?" and, now, this book "Disciple the Nations!" as texts for teaching their 1st and 2nd year students. And they will make this a compulsory subject in their academic programs.

Finally, the way Dr. Gross explains Luke 10, under the guidance of the Holy Spirit, is really awesome. His introducing the Harvest Prayer, Discovery Bible Study and Disciple Making Movements, touched the hearts of our people. And, very specifically, entering places by praying, "peace to this house," is truly a miracle-moment for evangelism according to the true teachings of the Lord Jesus Christ. I can now see how the early disciples lived, abiding in Christ and following His words, turning the whole world upside down. Why can't we see that today in Pakistan and everywhere?

In fact, we are beginning to see the same! I am experiencing, after praying "Peace to this house," the touching of many new hearts, just during this one month since Dr. Gross' visit. And I am not alone. Hundreds of leaders are sharing their testimonies that it has changed their practices and made it better in evangelizing different people groups.

So, I recommend this book to Christian leaders around the globe. It is a must-read book for your culture and context, and not only for Asia. May the Lord use it to help us reach the whole globe, paving the way for us to see the Book of Acts happening in our very own day!

Pastor Saqib Munawar
Founder & Chairman, C.A.N. Ministries

Preface

What Africa, the Holy Spirit and Pakistan taught me

For the last 11 years, I have been engulfed in the subject of New Testament Discipleship (NTD), realizing that it held the key to understanding both First Century Christianity and Christianity's global revival in our day. So, I have studied, taught, trained and written extensively on the allied themes of The Great Commission, Disciple Making Movements (DMMs), Discovery Bible Study (DBS), Healing Prayer and Revival.[1]

Africa

The places that the Lord had called Debby and me to focus on and serve, from early in our lives, were mainly Africa and the USA. So, I was surprised in 2018 when my African colleagues told me that they were committed to reaching their entire continent of 1 billion+ people with the gospel, making disciples of each and every culture group (nation/ethne). Adding, "we Africans have Africa covered. You are needed elsewhere, especially in your own country – the United States of America." Debby and I knew, from prayer and discussion, that they were right.

God was changing our basic call to serve Christ from one place to another. And in letting go of Africa, much elsewhere has been given room to arise. Over many years, Africa has taught me so much! It's people have embodied for us the biblical core values of community, the wisdom of elders, simplicity of lifestyle, extreme patience (longsuffering), boundless faith, and so much more. But,

---

[1] See my books at Amazon or for free e-copies at my website: www.disciplesgo.com   If you want an unpublished , FREE manuscript containing only significant quotes from 186 books related to NTD, then email me at ed.gross@comcast.net and simply state, "Send me the Quotes." This document is almost 500 pages long and will become a virtual library on NTD for your study and advancement in all things related to the Great Commission.

above everything, Africa has convinced me that Jesus, alone, is indispensable. That the Spirit of God really can do anything today, through any yielded vessel, anywhere. It was a thrilling moment of clarification for our mission call and our next steps.

The Holy Spirit

So, praying fervently for the Lord of the harvest to put us into His specific harvest field for us in the United States, the Lord began to lead us clearly. Always by praying and talking to esteemed colleagues, Deb and I were led by faith to move south from Philadelphia, deep into the state of Delaware. And there, having no contacts except Him, we were to focus our prayers and efforts in helping Disciple Making Movements[2] (DMMs) rise in each of the fourteen counties of Delmarva.[3]

By God's providential guidance we moved into the largest, very active retired community in Delmarva: Heritage Shores, in Bridgeville, DE. Our Philly home in Roxborough sold quickly and we rapidly left family and friends, moving 2 ½ hours south to Heritage Shores, with all its unknowns.

We began attending Bible-believing churches, looking for three dominant characteristics. (1) they were devotedly prayerful, (2) they were actively committed to Christian unity, desiring to work for the Kingdom rather than only their own local/denominational interests, and (3) they were open to change and to NT discipleship. We knew that without these three elements, a DMM cannot take root and grow. But it is not always easy to find prayer warriors, a humble, wide-hearted pastor, and a spirit willing to follow Jesus – all in the same place! Paul's problem was ours: *"For I have no one like him (Timothy), who will be genuinely concerned for your welfare. For they all seek their own interests, not those of Jesus Christ."*[4]

---

[2] A DMM is defined as 1000 new disciples made over a relatively brief period of time, in a specific region by up to 4 streams of disciplers, resulting in many new church plants and renewed churches.
[3] Delmarva is the Eastern shore area comprised of all of Delaware (3 counties), and parts of Maryland (9 counties) and Virginia (2 counties). A peninsula of nearly 1.5 million people, 170 miles long and up to 70 miles wide.
[4] Philippians 2:20-21

Soon, the Lord directed our path to Crossroad Community Church of Georgetown, DE. The ministry and friendship of CCC's amazing pastor, Rick Betts and of the saints there, met our three criteria. Little did we know that they had as much to offer us as we did, them! We found that it was in our mission to help Delmarva, that God greatly helped us, leading us forward into new vistas of growth and power in Christ.

Our 3 criteria were necessary; but, were not enough. I could not be used by the Lord Jesus to help catalyze DMMs without moving on to a much more powerful way of Christian living: *life in the Spirit.* I thought I was ready to be used of God and was considered by many as a mature servant of Christ. But, I still had some BIG holes in my life that needed to be filled.

Since our marriage in 1976, our lives had been fruitful, grounded in the Bible and in the Reformed Faith. But our experience, which was with various Reformed denominations all shared one big distinctive - they were not really open to the miraculous workings of the Holy Spirit.[5]

Without cramming some hardline viewpoint about Pentecost down our throats, Pastor Rick simply showed us what a thorough devotion to the Word of God, and to being filled with the Spirit looked like. While acknowledging the validity of NT discipleship and our ministry, he let me grow, at times recommending that I more deeply research the Holy Spirit in the Scriptures and in the biographies of men and women who were mightily used of God. He did this through long hours of sharing together. And by this patient approach, He helped me, showing me love – the chief fruit of the Holy Spirit.

Many months and hundreds of hours of research later, I simply could not deny the reality that it was God who had greatly and miraculously used people like Rick(today), and Andrew Murray, A J Gordon, Watchman Nee, John G Lake, Evan Roberts, Rees Howells, A B Simpson, William Seymour, Martyn Lloyd-Jones, and Brother Yun (the Heavenly man), name a few extraordinarily fruitful servants of the past. All of these, and countless others, believed,

---

[5] There were Reformed individuals who were exceptions to this, but they were rare instances

received, and taught the necessity of a post-conversion baptism with the Holy Spirit.

My own comprehensive study of the Word, together with their published biographies and works compelled me to become open and change. I had to recognize a reality that existed (and exists) outside of my own very limited experiences, studies and preferences. I could no longer deny the Holy Spirit His rightful place in my own and others' lives and ministries. The massive, scholarly works by Dr Jeff Oliver[6] and others clearly show that the miraculous gifts of the New Testament era have never ended.

It is a fact that the Holy Spirit has both naturally and supernaturally helped believers throughout world Christian history. From the time of Acts to today, millions of Christ-surrendered followers have enjoyed the New Testament-like influence of the Spirit. This great influence of the Spirit, occurring more or less, has been called many things by many believers throughout history: the baptism, a filling, a complete sanctifying, a second work of grace, an anointing, a divine empowering, a receiving of perfect love, an extraordinary power to witness of Christ, etc. Often by choosing a single expression or looking for a single outcome of the Spirit's presence and blessing, groups have gone somewhat astray and become unnecessarily divisive themselves. It is that tendency that I do not want to repeat here or elsewhere, ever. The sharp focus of this book is to declare that God is shalom. That the Father wants to unite His people under Christ by peace not pressure. By love not force. By the whole truth and not by merely partial truth – Christ, Himself being "the truth."

This paradigm shift produced many changes in our lives. But, the one huge benefit was that it clarified and revived our practical belief in the divine Trinity! We had never been anti-trinitarian theologically; but, practically speaking, my Trinity had long been: the Father, the Son and the Holy Scriptures! The Spirit

---

6 Jeff Oliver, Pentecost to the Present: The Holy Spirit's Enduring Work in the Church, 3 vols., Bridge Logos, Newberry, FL, 2017; See also The Century of the Holy Spirit: 100 Years of Pentecostal and Charismatic Renewal, by Vinson Synan, 2001, Thomas Nelson Publishers. 2000 Years of Charismatic Christianity by Dr Eddie Hyatt, Charisma House; Especially note the irenic works of Reformed Charismatic Dr Wayne Grudem.

had been absolutely limited to working through the words of the Bible. Now, the Triune foundation of the Father, the Son and the Holy Spirit has been re-established in our lives and ministry! Although, I would have never denied the reality of the person and work of the Spirit; I was not personally open to operating in the fullness of His ministry as seen on the pages of the New Testament. And so, His ability to use me was greatly hindered.

My former approach to the Bible had limited me from understanding the full gospel of the incarnated, crucified, risen and reigning Lord Jesus Christ. Operating in the full empowerment of the Holy Spirit can only come when the real, fully enthroned Jesus of TODAY is loved, exalted and obeyed. Think of it – I had been taught (and, so, taught others) to approach the Bible in a way that had resisted and grieved Its producer, the Holy Spirit, Himself! So, the Bible, by me, was used to repress its Author.[7] I am sure that I have offended many Bible-loving, Christ followers in the past by things I have said and written. And, in these ways, I have ignorantly enhanced division in the Body of Christ. For this and many similar sins, I ask God's and my fellow-believers' forgiveness. I truly want to be a man of peace, useful to the God of peace, in bringing both, healing to the Body, and hope to the lost.

Now my whole approach towards NT Discipleship has changed, because I no longer simply proclaim the biblical truth of it – but now enjoy and share the power of the Spirit, Himself, as I train others! I have begun calling my trainings: Spirit-Empowered Discipleship. The Lord has shown me that the miracles in the Book of Acts were not only activities of long-deceased Apostles, but the ongoing, current acts of the Holy Spirit. These are being seen and recorded through the DMMs that are today emerging globally by the power of the Spirit through obedient disciples of Jesus.[8]

---

[7] See 2 Peter 1:21; Mark 12:36; Acts 1:16; Hebrews 3:7
[8] As of Jan 2023, there are 1967 DMMs in open countries being carefully tracked globally, producing such a multiplication that the number of Christians in the world is doubling every 3.5 years!

Pakistan

Then Pakistan and Saqib Munawar were sent by God into my life. I had never been to Asia and had never met Saqib. But, somehow, he got a copy of my book, Are You a Christian or a Disciple? and was intrigued by the title. When he read it, he wrote to me and expressed very strongly that he believed that translating the book into Urdu, and distributing it to Christian leaders nationally, could be used by the Lord to create a much-needed paradigm shift in Pakistan. He believed this renewal could change church-going Christians into true disciples, called and empowered by Jesus who would make disciples by the power of the Spirit. This was in January of 2022, in the midst of the Covid Pandemic. I had not traveled abroad at all during Covid.

Saqib exhibited the most incredible persistence for this translation and publishing project. By His repeated requests, my hesitating heart was won over. Covid's economic horrors plus the awful flooding in Aug of 2022 created such poverty among many Pakistani Christians that the entire funding had to be raised through our USA contacts. The Lord blessed, and the money was procured for the translation and printing of 1000 copies. Then it became obvious that it would be better for me to visit for a ten-day intensive speaking tour throughout Eastern Pakistan. This would also require extensive funding to procure all the venues and help with the transportation and feeding of the many leaders coming to attend. God did it all.

However weird it might sound to you, in the midst of our planning, in November 2022, some demon tried to kill me in my bedroom one night while I was awake. A suffocating presence came into the room and swept all the air away. I found myself unable to breathe and simply cried out, "Leave, in the name of Jesus." Miraculously, immediately, the sinister presence left and normality was restored. The closer I got to going to Pakistan, the more Satan would oppose in numerous ways opened to him.

You see, Pakistan is the 5th largest country in the world, with an estimated population of 243 million. The nation's official name is the Islamic Republic of Pakistan. Kirachi is the most populated

Muslim city in the world, over 20 million people. Islam accounts for 97% of the population; Christianity 1.76%. The US State Department gave the country an American tourist rating of 3 out of 4, warning all USA citizens not to visit unless necessary. Level 4 is a demand not to visit. One week before leaving on the mission, there was a suicide bomber who killed 20+ at a police barracks in Karachi. The State Department advised me against traveling to Karachi. The city was one that we had planned to visit. Upon talking and praying, we decided to proceed cautiously with the plan.

Saqib is a 5th generation Christian. His father was a famous Christian educator and apologist. During our trip, through the ministry of the Word and Spirit, Saqib saw that God had a better way to reach Pakistan's lost millions than through skillful debate. He reminded me that the brilliant Pakistani Christian, Dr. KL Nasir, said on his deathbed, "I have won so many debates, but so few to Christ!" God did not send me to Pakistan to debate. Through his amazing organizing abilities, Saqib arranged for 6 large meetings over a 7-day period. I was in great health, for being nearly 70, and looked forward to day-long conferences during which I would teach (with Saqib translating) for 4-5 hours with one break.

The prayer support around the world was amazing – and truly was the key to the mission's success. We saw 1350 leaders introduced and trained in NT Discipleship and DMM. I returned home less than a week ago. The writing of this book is the result of focusing on the truths that were most used in stimulating renewal and life change through those meetings. That is why it is brief. Much more could be written and some has, being placed in the appendices at the end of the book. We are praying that its message will be blessed in the USA and throughout the Christian world, showing Christ's best way to fulfill His Great Commission – by individual and great movements of disciples working through peace not pressure.

Pakistan (and Saqib) has taught me that the Kingdom of God is at hand. That "one can still chase a thousand, and two, ten thousand"[9] for Christ's Kingdom! And that following Proverbs 1:23 together with Acts 2:37-39 by the Spirit can stir up renewal among

---

[9] See Deuteronomy 32:30

today's Christians. And this will lead to incredible multiplication, even the winning of whole countries by the Spirit-empowered obedience of today's new disciples. May this be your experience – and may Jesus Christ, alone, be exalted and followed, is our prayer.

"If you turn at my reproof, behold, I will pour out my Spirit to you; I will make my words known to you." (Proverbs 1:23 – Solomon)

"Now when they heard this they were cut to the heart, and said to Peter and the rest of the apostles, 'Brothers, what shall we do'" And Peter said to them, 'Repent and be baptized every one of you in the name of Jesus Christ for the forgiveness of your sins, and you will receive the gift of the Holy Spirit.'" (Acts 2:37-38 – Peter)

Ed Gross – March 2023

Part One
Discipleship – WHY?

Chapter One

Today's Democracies vs. Christ's Kingdom

"Now after John was arrested, Jesus came into Galilee, proclaiming the gospel of God, and saying, 'The time is fulfilled, and the kingdom of God is at hand; repent and believe the gospel.'" (Mark 1:14-15)

"But when the fullness of time had come, God sent forth his Son, born of a woman, born under the law, to redeem those who were under the law, so that we might receive adoption as sons" (Gal. 4:4).

Why would an old man like me go to Pakistan during a time when the US State Department advised against it? Why, with all the big books being written on discipleship today, is this one little book important? I will try to answer those important questions in Part One.

The Right Place and Time

Think of "the perfect moment" Paul was describing above in Galatians 4. That will help capture the meaning of "the fullness of time." Everything was ready. Judaism provided the Scriptures, a chosen nation and the dispersed synagogue system. Greek culture provided a universal, common language that permeated and united the whole Mediterranean world. And the Romans produced an unmatched time of peace (Pax Romana) through its Empire, a system of roads, waterways and viaducts that made transportation and water availability throughout the Mediterranean world at levels never before enjoyed. The Roman Empire also featured a both-and system of government that allowed compliant local governments to exist and even flourish, given certain stipulations. God had prepared the world for His Kingdom's coming through this fusion of unprecedented Jewish, Greek and Roman cultural/spiritual advancements. It was, indeed, *"the fullness of time."*

Jesus came when His Kingdom could spread quickly and widely. But there was one great governmental problem – the Roman Caesar was Lord. And he did not welcome rivals. In fact, the Caesars were notorious for eliminating rival powers. Christianity proclaimed, "Jesus is Lord," amid an Empire who suppressed that very claim.[10]

Why a Tyrannical Emperor?

So, please think about this – how could the timing of Messiah be *"perfect"* under a totalitarian ruler? Don't we think it would have been better had Jesus come much later, when democracies flourished, with all the blessings of civil liberty that we enjoy today? Shouldn't Paul have written, "But when things were almost perfect, God sent forth His Son..."?

No. Paul wrote as he was inspired by the Holy Spirit to write. He communicated the truth. The time was perfect. The setting was complete. Nothing needed to be added. Even the heavens declared this as, astronomically, the stars were in a perfect alignment, so that even astute pagan magi could see that something BIG was about to happen.[11]

I believe that the reality and power of the Kingdom of Christ are best portrayed against the backdrop of a totalitarian king like Caesar Augustus, rather than a US President or any other democratically-elected leader. What God intended to do in establishing Messiah's Kingdom would be best understood and embraced by those who were experiencing brutal, totalitarian Roman oppression. However, crazy it may sound, a form of monarchy prepared the way of Messiah better than a form of democracy. Or, said more relevantly, perhaps humbled, oppressed disciples in Pakistan, China and Iran can better understand submission to Christ, than Christians who enjoy a full range of civil liberties in the USA.[12]

---

[10] See Acts 17:6-7 and my "The Amazing Love of Paul's Model Church: How the Thessalonians became disciples and reached their region with the Gospel" (Parson's Porch Publishing, 2017).

[11] See the story of the Eastern Magi in Matthew 2:1-12

[12] Don't get me wrong – I am not saying that totalitarianism is a better form of government than is democracy. I am simply saying that Jesus is a King and deserves the total devotion and service of His Kingdom – His followers

Why? Because, though Jesus is as different as night is from day when compared to the Caesars, Jesus is still a king. In fact, He is the perfect, quintessential king. The King of kings. And fully understanding His Kingdom is impossible without understanding His total authority and unswerving law of love. Kings expect, even demand, obedience. Rebellion is not tolerated under a true monarchy. Jesus is not an exception to this norm. He calls His disciples, His Bride, His Church to obedience in the solemn final words of His Great Commission:

"Then Jesus came to them and said, 'All authority in heaven and on earth has been given to me. Therefore, go and make disciples of all nations, baptizing them in the name of the Father and of the Son and of the Holy Spirit, and teaching them to obey everything I have commanded you. And surely, I am with you always, to the very end of the age.'"[13]

Why few DMMs in the USA?

You see, there are many reasons why today's global reality of DMMs is not taking hold in the USA. One very significant reason is that the USA has become largely individualistic, drunken with the precious right to choose our officials – and ways of life. One of our greatest strengths has become a huge weakness. Personal rights, opinions and desires reign here. Personal selfishness, not selfless devotion to the community, is the ruling spirit of the age. We mock our Presidents, cherishing political cartoons more than honoring the office or its occupant. We vote them in and, just as easily, dismiss them. We Americans can hardly understand what Peter (and the Holy Spirit) meant when he reminded Jewish Christians everywhere to *"fear God, honor the king."*[14] With all our wonderful freedoms, we can hardly grasp either kingship or kingdom. So, we naturally misunderstand Jesus and the relationship we are to have with Him.

As nice as it is today, God knew that our political reality would have been a terrible backdrop for the emergence of God's

---

13 Matthew 28:18-20 (NIV)
14 1 Peter 2:17

Messiah, the Lord Jesus Christ. Today, we would not know a king if we saw one. But the resurrected Jesus actually reigns. He is not elected and cannot be dismissed. He can still call ten thousand angels, indeed the army of heaven, to do His bidding. Nebuchadnezzar had it right when he described the Kingdom of the God of Israel as follows:

> *"His dominion is an everlasting dominion, and his kingdom endures from generation to generation; all the inhabitants of the earth are accounted as nothing, and he does according to his will among the host of heaven and among the inhabitants of the earth; and none can stay his hand or say to him, "What have you done?"*[15]

The renowned Christian, Dietrich Bonhoeffer, clearly declared the spiritual demise of Western Christianity in his book, *The Cost of Discipleship*, when he wrote,

> "All along the line we are trying to evade the obligation of single-minded, literal obedience. How is such absurdity possible? What has happened that the word of Jesus can thus be degraded by this trifling, and thus left open to the mockery of the world? When orders are issued in other spheres of life there is no doubt whatever of their meaning. If a father sends his child to bed, the boy knows at once what he has to do. But suppose he has picked up a smattering of pseudo-theology. In that case he would argue more or less like this: 'Father tells me to go to bed, but he really means that I am tired, and he does not want me to be tired. I can overcome my tiredness just as well if I go out and play. Therefore, though father tells me to go to bed, he really means: Go out and play.' If a child tried such arguments on his father or a citizen on his government, they would both meet with a kind of language they could not fail to understand—in short, they would be punished. Are we

---

[15] Daniel 4:34-35

to treat the commandment of Jesus differently from other orders and exchange single-minded obedience for downright disobedience? How could that be possible?"[16]

We need to consider such strong words today as we, in the West, tend to exalt individualism, choosing a comfortable, selfish and materialistic way of life that is interrupted by occasional visits to church and bursts of Christian service. And, from this, our spiritual weakness, we draw the plans and strategies for evangelizing the rest of the world. How well have they done?

We must recognize that the Roman empire, its Caesar and intimidating army, made a perfect setting for the coming of Christ according to the Holy Spirit. How? Simply because God does not desire that anyone should ever make the mistake that "asking Jesus into one's heart" could be a matter of enjoying the salvation Jesus offers without bowing to Him and serving Him as his Lord. Yet countless Westernized Christians are today making that very mistake.

This is the dilemma that American Christianity has created. We have idolized our rights and dethroned the one Master of the Universe-Jesus. But there was no such dilemma in the First Century.

NT Discipleship–Hard to Grasp Today in the USA

Jews living at the time of Jesus understood the terms of His call, for they were the terms of total subjection. No one could follow Jesus as a disciple and demand his own rights, for Jesus unequivocally and repeatedly said to all,

"If anyone would come after me, let him deny himself and take up his cross daily and follow me. For whoever would save his life will lose it, but whoever loses his life for my sake will save it. For what does it profit a man if he gains the whole world and loses or forfeits himself?"[17]

---

[16] Bonhoeffer, the Cost of Discipleship, p 90
[17] Luke 9:23-25; 14:26-27; John 12:24-25

When Jesus chose to liken being His disciple with bearing one's cross, He was speaking their language. Their roads were lined with the crucified bodies of their fellow countrymen who bore their crosses to their places of execution. To where they would die. They had somehow challenged and defied Rome and they must pay the cost.

This is why we must consider what it means to be a disciple of Jesus today. Because the very concept of discipleship is hard to grasp. A true follower commits to more than attending church on occasion. We need to wrestle with whether it is even possible in a country like the USA to conceive of Jesus as our King. I truly wonder if Paul or Peter would even recognize our churches as the products of their teachings! We need to repent!

Why I went to Pakistan

That is why I went to Pakistan. To make sure that they understand the terms of their King Jesus. To make sure they did not begin to wander down our Western path of idolized individualism. To tell them I am sorry and to help undo any remnants of decisional evangelism, replacing them with discipleship evangelism. To remind them of the Way of Jesus – a plan of salvation by peace not pressure. And they saw it immediately!

You see, in Pakistan, China or other countries where Christians are a despised and persecuted minority, they understand the concept of absolute rule because they have lived under it. So, when I preached NT Discipleship to them, which demands their submission, there was no issue. They were never a totally free people, anyways. The discipleship call of Jesus, to Christians in persecution, isn't demanding too much.

Unfortunately, such is not now the case in the USA. Democracy, cut loose from law, has taken a bad turn here. Christ's terms of discipleship are being rejected by many Western Christians today. And so, the great movements of discipleship spreading so quickly elsewhere, have ground to a halt in America before hardly starting. The Kingdom of God that is spreading through DMMs has met its match! Where? Not in jihadist Islam, or in atheistic

Communism, or in radicalized Hinduism, or in shamanistic Animism – but in Americanized Christianity! It seems that we have chosen to ask a Jesus into our hearts that, somehow, we do not have to follow or obey! And for this there are horrible consequences in our lives, our homes, our churches and our cultures. Consider the warning behind the note of Matthew, which he must have written with amazement, of his all-powerful Savior, the incarnate Son of God, *"And he did not do many miracles there because of their lack of faith."*[18]

But, thanks be to God, He still has room for American Christians, as He does for anyone. But, we must allow for the dashing, the complete makeover of our idol - America's perversely, individualized and hyper-democratized Christianity - through the unchanging terms of the Spirit as given through Solomon (Proverbs 1) and Peter (Acts 2). The Kingdom of God is still at hand in our land, if we will believe, surrender to King Jesus and begin to obey Him like little children.

---

[18] Matthew 13:58 (NIV)

Chapter Two

Today's DMMs vs. the Blood of the Martyrs

Before showing the incredible manner that the Kingdom of Christ is advancing today, by peace rather than pressure, I must make sure that you understand how important, how vital this subject of disciple making is for us all. And, so, I am mentioning a couple big impediments that we have lying before us that must be removed. In chapter one, we saw how our culture's unparalleled freedom can be at the same time our great strength and a great weakness. Another problem results from our unknowingly replacing Jesus' mission strategy in a very subtle but deadly way.

Martyrdom – Not God's Norm

Faith is at war with fear within every follower of Jesus. And one fear-- that of imminent martyrdom-- certainly can and has often impeded the spread of Christianity. True, the testimonies of some who have died for their faith has had a lifechanging impact on some of their onlookers. But, I want to make it clear that though some may be called to martyrdom – that is NOT the norm. Physically dying for Jesus is not the revealed will of God for the host of His Gospel-sharing children. Unfortunately, this truth has not been taught until very recently. And as a result, many of Christ's followers in persecuted lands have grown quiet.

Tertullian, one of the famous Christian Apologists (155-220AD), is quoted as having made a statement that has become almost biblical in its being generally accepted as truth by today's Christians: "The blood of the martyrs is the seed of the Church."[19]

I must tread very carefully here because there are many great Christian non-profits and churches which raise large sums of money

---

[19] Excerpted from The Apologeticus (written ca 197 AD), by Tertullian of Carthage in Northern Africa, which was a treatise very ably defending Christianity written to the provincial governors of the Roman Empire and the magistrates of Carthage.

to care for martyrs' families. And I do not want to diminish their loving ministries. There is a danger, though, of turning martyrdom into a discipling strategy for today's millions of Christians living in persecuting cultures. Jesus taught that all godly followers will be persecuted.[20] But, that does not mean all will or should die for their faith. Let me carefully explain.

In my recent trip to Pakistan, I found that when I declared, with exegetical precision and spiritual power, that Jesus does NOT want His followers to unnecessarily risk their lives by their witness – there was universal relief. Hundreds of my listeners were instantly renewed by the promises of their Savior that He would be with them and protect them, as He always has His people, with very few exceptions. And that He clearly established a way to disciple nations by peace not pressure. They began to be filled with hope.

While I was researching this chapter, I accessed a very helpful Christianity Today article that was written 8 years ago entitled, "Sorry Tertullian."[21] The conclusions of both the author, Morgan Lee, and the major contributor, Justin Long, were "recent research tests the most famous adage about the persecuted church." Long "believes persecution initially harms churches because it interrupts networks and promotes emigration." Historian Stuart George Hall noted that the word "Church" is not even in Tertullian's original quote, and said, "Their blood is not so much the seed of the church as the seed of virtuous living and dying." Long's research concluded that "Church growth is not strongly correlated with either governmental or societal persecution."

Our Safety truly Matters to Christ

These conclusions were exactly what mine and many others recently have been, simply from reading and following the disciple making strategy Jesus used when He sent the 72 out in Luke 10. Today's greatest mission strategy is simply to obey the spirit and form of how Jesus made disciples. To follow His commands like little children. And, as we will see in Part Three, that form reminded

---

20 See John 15:20; 2 Timothy 3:12
21 Christianity Today, Dec 4, 2014

those who were sent out on mission that He was *"sending you out as lambs in the midst of wolves."*[22] He had earlier warned the 12 Apostles that they should be *"wise as serpents and harmless as doves."*[23] He was now expanding that warning to the 72. Jesus wanted them to know that His presence with them and His going before them was that of a tender God who loved and would always care for them and their families. I wish you could have seen how this message brought tremendous encouragement to the persecuted minority of Pakistan!

Just a few days ago, I read a very helpful article sent out by DMMs Frontier Missions entitled, "5 Things that Destroy Discipleship Movements." These are sometimes called "death factors." Well, number 3 is entitled: Fear of Persecution, and includes these warnings:

> "Fear of persecution is very contagious. Sadly, fear is often a major issue in the lives of cross-cultural missionaries trying to initiate movements. Missionaries are told they need to be careful to not do anything that would cause them to lose their visas to stay in a country. Consequently, cautious missionaries impart the same DNA to those they disciple."

As I will soon explain in Part Two -- how we missionaries read or hear the biblical commands of Jesus determines everything. If we read Luke 10 as merely Western Christian analysts 2000 years after Jesus gave those commands, we will readily mess with them. We will alter their content, softening their clear demands. We missiologists routinely excuse ourselves by saying that we are "contextualizing" the commands. In fact, could we really be disobeying the very commands we are supposed to be promoting, likely because we do not have the faith to obey them, ourselves? We all too often respond like 21st century Christians, rather than like the first hearers, the original disciples, who would have heard them, memorized them and obeyed them verbatim.

Of course, great courage is needed by both speaker and listener whenever we are delivering a message demanding

---

[22] Luke 10:3 and Matthew 10:16
[23] Matthew 10:16b

repentance. That is because people do not like to change and that we will do anything other than change, if it's at all possible.[24] We are naturally stubborn and proud. All of us. So, the command to repent, is meant to cut each of us to the heart. It's a command for us all.

We must be careful to think through our strategy even when we are trying to help others. Nik Ripken, in his shockingly honest book, The Insanity of God, returned from Somalia to the USA a broken man, and tearfully wrote,

> "After all the time, the expense, the energy, and the sacrifice expended by so many people, what (if anything) had our years in Somalia really accomplished? ...For six long, hard, dry years we had watched and waited.... But how and when could those seeds ever grow? Who would be there to reap the harvest – if there ever was a harvest? .... Where in Somalia is the good soil? Is there any good soil? Could a seed ever grow here? .... What could we have done differently? What should we have done differently?"[25]

It took years, but God began showing Nik, and many missionaries with him, a new path. Tremendous light has emerged from those dark nights of the soul.

When we Follow Christ's Plan

Another missionary, David Watson, helps explain what God showed him in a similarly dark time of life. Not all mission strategy is good strategy. There can be bad strategy, too. Like David Watson described so painfully in the beginning chapter of his landmark book, Contagious Disciple Making. This is what he wrote,

> "'God, I can't plant churches anymore. I didn't sign on to love people, train people, send people, and get them killed.' Six men I had worked with had been martyred over the last

---

[24] See Trousdale and Sunshine's brilliant chapters in "The Kingdom Unleashed," (2018) on the Dannemiller formula for change.
[25] Nik Ripkin (not real name), The Insanity of God, pp 135-136

eighteen months…. (I cried), 'Take away my call. I will go back to the States. I'm good at business. I will give lots of money to missions. Let someone else plant churches. Release me from my call.' Every day for two months we had the same conversation. Every day I went to my office, sat in the dark and begged God to take away my call. He refused.'

"Fine, You have to teach me how to plant churches…. Show me in Your Word how you want me to reach these people. If you show me, I will do it. This was my covenant with God."[26]

The rest of the story is still being told. But, as David's team discovered and followed the original strategy of Jesus, as revealed in Luke 10, the Holy Spirit birthed a Disciple Making Movement in northern India that is still multiplying today. With over 1,000 churches being planted in the fifth year of employing this strategy! All this in the Indian area known as "the graveyard of missions and missionaries." My Pakistani audiences, just two weeks ago listened with shock and joy as I declared to them this truth! India borders Pakistan. Of course, they began praying – "If there, here, too, Lord!"

The blood of the martyrs almost sent David Watson home in a state of depression. It was, to him and many like him, the opposite of "the seed of the Church." But, glory to God, I heard Watson declare a few years ago that he, alone, introducing and training leaders in the principles of DMMs, has seen well over 50 DMMs launched by the Spirit globally. In fact, there are presently 1967 DMMs being carefully tracked in countries where accountability is possible![27]

The Danger of Exporting our Evangelistic Styles

You can only imagine the dangers and difficulties that have come from simply exporting Western styled evangelism to these

---

[26] David and Paul Watson, Contagious Disciple Making,(2014) xi-xiii.
[27] See Frontiers magazine's entire issue for Jan/Feb 2023! Closed countries like China, Iran etc., have many DMMs flourishing within them, but they simply cannot be tracked carefully and added to these incredible numbers

countries. Our sharing the gospel within a free, largely non-threatening culture, has been an unusual luxury in world history. I was an Evangelism Explosion trainer and used it in church plants in the USA. Before that I was trained with the early Billy Graham evangelistic movies, where multitudes went forward after their viewing in a theater. And before that a bold witness in the John R Rice, Sword of the Lord, school of boldness mode, where we were taught that "evangelistic unction is more caught than taught." Just do it! So, we would run into houses with our Bibles just like firemen ran into burning buildings with their hoses. This was not unusual in the 70's in the USA!

But our successes in our free land just did not parallel the realities of the First Century witnesses or many today who live as minorities within radically opposing cultures. Of course, all is now changing in the USA, as culture today is becoming hostile to Christianity. But, we just haven't pivoted well and, instead of re-appraising our strategies, we have largely exported them. Until the recent, undeniable reality of DMMs!

Our old door to door and mass evangelism strategies no longer bear as much *"fruit that remains"* at home. And they simply increase the pressures on those we are training in evangelism abroad. What I am here clearly claiming is that when I went door to door and put my foot rudely in someone's door so they could not close it – until I had sufficiently warned them of the wrath to come – I was doing what I had been taught NOT what Jesus did. And, as I look back, this approach should not have been characterized as either biblical or courageous. It was, in fact, largely unbiblical and poorly reflected on our Savior and His tender saving love. Yes, I was well-intentioned; but, it did much harm, while doing some good.

When those or similar tactics are employed in a Christian persecuted minority culture, devastating results can happen. But, when our God of love's strategy for reaching the lost is literally followed, what we see is many more people saved and many less martyrs made.

Martyrdoms in Acts

It is estimated that Acts 1-12 covers a span of about thirteen years. And how many martyrdoms are mentioned in the inspired history? Though the Church was started at Pentecost, in the very teeth of the lion (Jerusalem), when it served the Sanhedrim best to extinguish the new Christian movement, there are only two recorded martyrdoms: Stephen (Acts 7) and James (Acts 12). Yes, there was persecution – but it was used, as it always is, to refine disciples and to redistribute trained disciples to new areas. You see, Jesus gave the command to flee from severe persecution.[28] It is interesting that in today's Underground Church in China, missionaries are trained how to jump out of windows and escape when the secret police are hunting them down! Brother Yun the heavenly man, called this type of evangelistic training, "fleeing evangelism."[29]

When we read the missionary history of Acts, it seems as though one great purpose in writing those accounts was to reveal the many miraculous escapes, deliverances, advances of the gospel, and answers to prayer that routinely marked the lives of those first disciples. What is God trying to show us, today when we study Acts? Is it that the blood of the martyrs is the best way to advance church growth and planting? Obviously not. It is to show us how Jesus is with us to the end of the age. And this Jesus, this God, loves, protects and uses His humble people in their efforts to make disciples by the power of the Holy Spirit – with peace rather than pressure.

So, whether it is in the West or in the 10/40 Window, the Word of Christ is applicable because Christ reigns! *"Heaven and earth will pass away, but my words will not pass away."*[30]

---

[28] See Matthew 10:23; 24:16 and Revelation 12:14
[29] See The Heavenly Man, by Paul Hattaway, pp 55ff
[30] Matthew 24:35

Chapter Three

Today's Evangelical Churches and Repentance

The Beauty of an Extended Family

During my recent trip to Pakistan, I was hosted by a very busy yet prayerful Christian leader. His ministry took him throughout Asia and the Middle East. Into many dangerous places with great challenges.[31] What did I notice about his home? His elderly, godly mother lived with him, as did his disabled but immensely talented sister, his wife and four children. And during my three visits to his home – these were never the only believers in his home. There always were others. Others praying and eating with us. And the home was a center of praise. Of peace not pressure!

Saqib and Sheba embraced their extended biological family, as well as their extended Christian family. And my hours with them demanded the same of me – if I was to become a part of their biblical way of living. This way of life is an almost never chosen lifestyle among American Evangelicals. Why? Because it opposes "the American dream" of a large, spacious home, away from the noise and disturbances of the city, with a two-car garage opened and closed by a remote, welcoming us into the self-absorbed, quiet existence of comfort, filled with the many pleasant distractions which we can indulge whenever we desire. The "American dream" of the kids and grandkids being just far enough away to visit and leave when convenient. The "American dream" of life without community, without interruptions, without getting too involved in others' lives and "issues."

I am sure that my Pakistani host and his family also must deal with sin daily. But I am only writing what I saw. Of the way of

---

[31] Like rescuing 53 orphans who had been born to mothers who had been raped by Taliban forces, and who were forced to leave their children so that they could survive, themselves.

life that I was surrounded by. Of a 12-year-old, first-born son who was brought into his daddy's cramped office quarters to take part in their washing my feet. Literally. Because the Jesus of John 13 had passed on a practice that He then commanded His followers to do. And by doing this, to show their love for one another, proving the reality of their being disciples of Jesus.

Hungry Disciples or Overfed Christians?

In Pakistan, I was absorbed and challenged by a new way of life. I was deeply greeted everywhere I was taken. With rose petals, garlands of flowers, pieces of traditional clothing to wear, always plenty of pure, spring water to drink. And plenty of smiles and singing! At times individuals would come forward and hand me wrapped-up gifts (which my nervous body guards took and tested to make sure they were not package bombs—and none were, PTL!).

Each of my addresses was 4-5 hours long, which they respectfully took in, many taking notes, and no one running off to the bathroom. I was as amazed by how they listened as they were with what the Spirit gave me to share with them. I had not seen such hunger for the truth of the Word and its teachings on discipleship in much of the West. I have seen some, and am thankful for it. But, in Pakistan, it was virtually everyone.

My writings on NT discipleship have only opened a few doors to me in the USA. In fact, they have shut many doors. In Pakistan, they had opened up everything, everywhere! I was there because Saqib had picked up one of my books in a bookstore in another Asian country. Read it. And had his life transformed by responding to the conviction of the Spirit of truth. He knew that His hungry Pakistani brothers and sisters were eager for the truth that Jesus promised would set them free.[32]

But freedom is a ten-cent word in the USA. And increasingly fewer see the beauty of it, not realizing that, swimming in personal rights, many are drowning in an enslaving lifestyle of

---

[32] See John 8:31-32

selfishness. Our Lord had already clearly declared the hard truth we try to ignore, "*You cannot serve God and money.*"[33]

Discipleship's First Word – Repent!

Before turning to the message that persecuted Pakistani Christians were longing for, I must share just one more urgent message with my American readers. "*Repent, for the kingdom of heaven is at hand.*"[34]

Please remember this - we must change. We must choose to change. The Spirit of God will pass us by in today's global renewal, if we do not repent. The only way Judaism could be ready for the coming Messiah was for a forerunner to declare, "*I baptize you with water for repentance, but he who is coming after me is mightier than I, whose sandals I am not worthy to carry. He will baptize you with the Holy Spirit and fire.*"[35] And they repented! Whole crowds of ordinary people from Judea and Jerusalem, with tax collectors and soldiers among them, were crying out in repentance for the forgiveness of sins.[36] And to them all, John preached, "*Bear fruit in keeping with repentance!*"[37]

God has made it clear that our words and prayers of repentance are a sham without a corresponding life change. If Jesus were to return, as many USA Christians are hoping, would He demand anything of us? Or just catch us all up in the air, because we are justified by faith? Does that make us ready if it is standing alone in our lives? Is there no danger of being like the five virgins who "*went to meet the bridegroom*," but "*they took no oil with them, while the wise took flasks of oil with their lamps.*"[38] Don't you recall the rest of that parable? "*As the bridegroom delayed…at midnight there was a cry, 'Here is the bridegroom! Come out to meet him.'*" As they trimmed their lamps, the foolish ones futilely begged for oil, ran off to buy some and missed his arrival. To these unready, oil-less virgins Jesus said, "*Truly, I say*

---

33 Luke 16:13
34 Matthew 3:2
35 Matthew 3:11-12
36 Mark 1:4-5; Luke 3:10-16
37 Matthew 3:8; Luke 3:8
38 Matthew 24:3-4

to you, I do not know you." And to all His listeners, added this warning, *"Watch therefore, for you do not know neither the day nor the hour."*[39]

I am afraid that many of us in the USA have been rocked to sleep by much of today's preaching. Certainly, we think that we are ready for His return. We cannot be like the foolish virgins. We have sound doctrine! We attend church! We give good money every week or two! We go on mission trips!

Time to take Inventory

To the churches of his day, Peter warned, *"For it is time for judgment to begin at the household of God: and if it begins with us, what will be the outcome for those who do not obey the gospel of God? And if the righteous is scarcely saved, what will become of the ungodly and the sinner?"*[40]

Paul warned the spiritually-gifted Corinthians, *"Examine yourselves, to see whether you are in the faith. Test yourselves."*[41] And Jesus warned us all, *"Not everyone who says to me, 'Lord, Lord' will enter the kingdom of heaven. But the one who does the will of my Father in heaven. On that day many will say to me, 'Lord, Lord did we not prophesy in your name, and cast out demons in your name, and do many mighty works in your name?' And then will I declare to them, 'I never knew you; depart from me, you workers of lawlessness.'"*[42]

The reason you need this book is because only few of you know the way of Christ, which happens to be the path of NT Discipleship. Though all of you know the way to church. And you affirm that you are a Christian. Maybe even a "born again" or "Bible-believing" Christian; but, you have no clue whether you are a true disciple or not.

Our danger is real and it is this: Jesus called disciples and commanded them, *"Go and make disciples of all the nations"* in the Great Commission that we all would say we believe and love. BUT we do not know HOW to make a disciple. All we know is HOW to make church-going Christians. And millions will likely stand before Jesus

---

[39] Matthew 24:5-13
[40] 1 Peter 4:17-18
[41] 2 Corinthians 13:5
[42] Matthew 7:21-23

in judgment--unprepared, without oil--because they were Christians and not disciples or followers of Jesus! It just happened to be that fact which Saqib read of in my book which led him to request me to have translated into Urdu, the language of his country. He had repented of this disciple-less Christianity and had begun to see the fruit of a real renewal of biblical discipleship in his life and ministry.[43]

When MOST Churches needed to Repent

We have been taught to view repentance as the duty of non-Christians in order to be saved. Are Christians really called to repent? It is hard for us in the West to even conceive of whole Christian churches crying out in repentance. But, this is exactly what Jesus demanded of five out of the seven churches of Asia to whom He sent little letters AFTER He had risen, ascended and begun His reign in heaven! As you read those seven short messages,[44] you had better do so on your knees. Because those which He demanded, "REPENT," were far better, more obedient and faithful than are many Evangelical churches today!

Those five churches were not marked with the same levels of freedom, comfort, disposable time, recreational distractions, internet information, cable TV, mobility and fast-food, etc. that is normal of today's Western Christians. YET, Jesus specifically pointed out what they MUST repent of.[45] 5 out of 7 = 71% of the churches! In the 1st century. And here we are, 21 centuries later, and we think it is only others who need to repent and begin living differently. God, help us turn again to Prov. 1:23!

Please, I am about to expose the chasm between you and NT era disciples, in Part Two. Yet, many of you read your New Testaments like you belong there. Like you are believing and doing today what they believed and did in the NT era. Reading it does not make it so! We read Acts just like we are part of the same Body as

---

[43] I am only dealing with a fraction of the book Saqib read, Are you a Christian or a Disciple?, which exposes Western Christianity's rejection of Lordship salvation and discipleship, in its 322 pages, 205 footnotes, and 5 appendices.
[44] Revelation 2:1-3:22
[45] See Rev. 2:4-5; 2:16; 2:20-22; 3:1-3; 3:15-19

they are. With a similar devotion, faith and fruitfulness. John the Baptist warns us: *"His (Jesus') winnowing fork is in his hand, and he will clear his threshing floor and gather the wheat into the barn, but the chaff he will burn with unquenchable fire."*[46]

Please, hear from Jesus, Himself, who warned His sympathetic followers, *"Do you think that the 18 on whom the tower in Siloam fell ... were worse sinners than all the others who lived in Jerusalem? No, I tell you; but unless you repent, you will all likewise perish."*[47] The believers in Pakistan repented in hearing the truth that you are about to hear. Will you?

---

[46] Matthew 3:12
[47] See Luke 13:1-5

Part Two
Discipleship – WHAT?

Chapter Four

Are you a Christian or a Disciple?

I hope that you will become, like Timothy, by God's grace, *"a vessel for honor, sanctified and useful for the Master, prepared for every good work."*[48] I cannot help you if I dilute my words on this subject. I will write to you as frankly as I spoke to my Pakistani audiences. I knew that I likely had only one opportunity to speak to each of them. And I only will have your attention for a short time. So, here is what I asked them – and ask you:

> *-How many of you are Christians?* (virtually everyone raised a hand)

> *-How many of you believe and love the Great Commission of Jesus, which is His final command to "Go and disciple the nations?"* (same response)

This is what I have asked Christian groups when I am introducing NT discipleship to them. Everywhere. Always with a nearly unanimous show of hands. But then I look at them concerned, sometimes weeping, and ask,

> *-So, how many disciples have you made?* (a look of shame, shock, or offense results)

Immediately, the Holy Spirit grips my hearers with this convicting truth. What good is it to say we believe in something – even publicly – and then realize that there is no evidence for our belief? To declare that we support the Great Commission, with its goal of making disciples everywhere, while we, ourselves are making none! So that you do not think I am overstepping this line of questioning, remember Jesus asked His disciples, *"Why do you call me, 'Lord, Lord'*

---

[48] 2 Timothy 2:21 (NKJV)

and do not do what I tell you?"[49] Psychologists have a clinical word for patients with "beliefs" that have no basis in reality. They don't call them "beliefs," they call them "delusions!"[50] And the person, then, is noted as delusional.

When a Megachurch Pastor Repented

The pastor of the then-fifth largest church in the USA (20,000+ members), when repenting of his own devotion to decisional evangelism (with every head bowed...repeat this prayer) and his neglect of discipleship evangelism (If anyone would come after me..."), told his stunned audiences that he was sorry that he had made them fervent fans worshiping Jesus on Sunday mornings, rather than making them faithful followers of Jesus throughout the week![51] He admitted to them all,

> "Too often in my preaching I have tried to talk people into following Jesus. I wanted to make following him as appealing, comfortable, and convenient as possible. And I want to say that I am sorry."[52]

As he continued down that discipleship way, he lost 25% of his members. They had not signed-up to follow Jesus. They had conveniently asked Him into their lives and had quickly assigned Him a place in the corner of the back porch. They wanted to go to heaven when they died; but did not want to be too heavenly-minded while they lived.

When the Spirit "Spoke" to me

I can remember exactly when that truth first gripped my soul. I was carefully teaching through Acts at a Bible College in South Africa in 2011. I had leaders and future leaders of 25+ African countries eagerly watching, listening and taking notes. And I realized

---

49 Luke 6:46
50 See Kyle Idleman, Not a Fan, p. 106
51 For the stunning story see, Not a Fan by Kyle Idleman, Zondervan, 2011
52 Idleman, Not a Fan, p 14

44

that I was not on the same path as those early Christians! When reading of Luke's use of "*disciple*" when writing of believers, that the first Christians began their walk with Jesus as utterly devoted followers. Not as "baby Christians" who would slowly ramp up into becoming disciples. And the Holy Spirit whispered a life changing statement and question into my spirit,

"You are not fulfilling the Great Commission the way that the Apostles did. Who do you think is right?"

So, in the Spring of 2011, before my God, my wife and my students, I began what has become an absolutely consuming quest ever since:

-To discover what the Bible says about disciples
-To discover what the word "disciple" meant when used by Jesus and others
-To research comprehensively what Christian authors have written and taught on this all-important subject
-To follow Jesus every day with new repentance and faith
-To share with everyone the results of my research

Little did I know that during that time, and for some years, there were literally hundreds of Christians having the same wrestling of spirit and coming to the same conclusions all around the globe! The Lord was moving His Church! Much of my research has been written down and is available for free to Christians wanting to fulfill the Great Commission today.[53] I briefly summarize some of these truths I have discovered in Appendix One. Many others have discovered the same and more!

Denominationalized not Discipled

If you have never been discipled, it is unlikely that you are a disciple. If you have been shown how to become a Christian, you have been Christianized. Or, more likely, denominationalized. The

---

[53] Just email me at ed.gross@comcast.net and say – Send me the Quotes and I will send you the most recent edition

difference matters because Jesus invited all who would be saved to follow Him, which was the rabbinic way a Rabbi would invite someone to become His disciple.

Becoming a denominational Christian also matters to God because Jesus taught against unnecessary sectarianism,[54] and prayed for unity in later Christianity, opposing denominational factions.[55]

Please do not misunderstand me. I am not saying that if one is ignorant of how to become a disciple, only being shown how to become a Christian, that he cannot be saved. That is a matter of heart and is also known perfectly only to God. Jesus said, *"he who is not against us is on our side."*[56] In 1966, I was among many who, then, received Jesus by faith without knowing His call to discipleship. We desired with all our hearts to surrender our lives to Him, beginning to share our faith with others. We did not invite Him into our lives on our terms, but His – as best we knew them.

No Cost Salvation

But, over the years, many in the West have been invited to salvation with no self-denial, no cost and no fruit. And the results have been devastating both in their lives and in the churches. Bishop JC Ryle (1816-1900), renowned for his warm evangelical faith and clear biblical thinking, wrote during a time of spiritual decline,

> "Very likely your religion costs you nothing. Very probably it neither costs you trouble, nor time, nor thought, nor care, nor pains, nor reading, nor praying, nor self-denial, nor conflict, nor working, nor labor of any kind…. Such a religion as this will never save your soul…. A religion that costs nothing is worth nothing."[57]

---

[54] Luke 9:49-50
[55] John 17:9-11, 20-23
[56] Luke 9:50
[57] Ryle quoted in James Boice, Christ's Call to Discipleship, 1986, p. 112

True or False Grace?

If that was true 150 years ago, it is even more so today. But, today we hear cries of, "What about God's grace?" And "That sounds a lot like salvation by works!" May these words of Dietrich Bonhoeffer suffice,

> "Cheap grace is the deadly enemy of our Church. We are fighting today for costly grace.... Cheap grace is grace without discipleship... Costly grace is the treasure hidden in the field; for the sake of it a man will gladly go and sell all that he has.... Such grace is *costly* because it calls us to follow, and it is *grace* because it calls us to follow Jesus Christ. It is *costly* because it costs a man his life, and it is *grace* because it gives a man the only true life."[58]

Make no mistake, my friends, we believe salvation is by grace through faith. But, far too many today think in this manner,

> "My only duty as a Christian is to leave the world for an hour or so on a Sunday morning and go to church to be assured that my sins are all forgiven. I need no longer to try to follow Christ, for cheap grace, the bitterest foe of discipleship, which discipleship must loathe and detest, has freed me from that."[59]

It is out of love that I ask you to ask yourself, am I Christian or a Disciple? 2.3 billion people claim to be Christians. How many of them follow Jesus? How many of them have heard His invitation and, truly, responded with all their hearts? *"Come to me, all who labor and are heavy laden, and I will give you rest. Take my yoke upon you, and learn from me, for I am gentle and lowly in heart, and you will find rest for your souls. For my yoke is easy and my burden is light."*[60] NT experts have said that the invitation to "take my yoke upon you" was a commonly used

---

[58] Bonhoeffer, The Cost of Discipleship, pp 45-47
[59] Bonhoeffer, The Cost of Discipleship, pp 54-55
[60] Matthre 11:228-29

phrase of NT era rabbis when they invited others to become their disciples. How many of the 2.3 billion know that the Matthew 11:28 invitation is not merely given for one to be saved? It is given to all to become disciples of Jesus. As we now turn to defining that word as He did in the NT era, I pray that you may answer THAT question both accurately and honestly. Because how you answer, Are **YOU** a Christian or a Disciple?, is critical for time and for eternity.

Chapter Five

The Marks of a New Testament Disciple 1

Since, Jesus did not command the Church to make Christians, but to make disciples, it is a matter of first importance to make sure that we know what the word "disciple" meant in the NT era. Rather, many are arguing over what it means to be a "true Christian." Though I am not pushing for us to lay aside that word, no less a global church leader than the late John Stott said, while addressing national leaders at the National Prayer Breakfast in Washington, DC,

> "The word 'Christian' occurs only three times in the Bible. Because of its common misuse we could profitably dispense with it. Jesus Christ and the Apostle Paul never used the word, at least not in their recorded teaching."[61]

We must not make the mistake of assuming that because the words "disciple" and "discipleship" are being used much more in today's Christian strategies and writings, that those using the words mean what Jesus and other rabbis meant when they used the words. The sad fact is that most today do not know what Jesus and his contemporary rabbis meant by those words. Truly, most today, do not mean what those in the 1st century meant when using those words. This misappropriating of good, biblical terms by many today is easily revealed by simply quoting what the Bible says and comparing it to what many current Christians today are saying and writing.[62]

The State of Discipleship in the USA

In this short book, I will quote what the "executive summary" was when the Barna Group was employed by the

---

[61] John Stott in the summer 2007 issue of Knowing and Doing
[62] See the first four chapters of "Are you a Christian or a Disciple" (pp19-66)

Navigators to determine "The State of Discipleship" in the USA.[63] In the first sentence of the "executive summary" of their research, they admit,

> "a critical component of this study is to *define* 'discipleship.' The concept is familiar to many, but a widely accepted definition remains elusive."[64]

Bingo! After spending untold thousands of dollars to do the research, Barna and the Navigators concluded that people are TODAY generally confused about what Jesus meant when He commanded us, to go and make disciples!

Why is it so difficult to get an agreeable definition when the word is one of the most repeated nouns describing a believer in the New Testament? Perhaps it is because doing a comprehensive study, as we have done, will demand a significant paradigm shift or life change by US who call ourselves Christians! Saqib understood this and, so, invited me to Pakistan. Not to get money from the West. Not to add glory to his position. But, to help catalyze a paradigm shift among all Christians in Pakistan!

So that you understand that this is not just me making a conclusion that does not speak well of the spiritual condition of most Evangelicals in the USA, the Barna/Navigators summary declares, "Christian adults and church leaders alike most commonly prefer 'becoming Christ-like' to describe the process of spiritual growth (rather than discipleship)."[65] In other words, let's not study the Bible comprehensively (all 250+ instances), declaring precisely what IT says, and DO it with the help of the Spirit. Instead, let's scrap "discipleship" and replace it by the phrase "becoming more Christ-like." Well, look around and see how well that short-cut strategy has worked. Jesus did not say, "If anyone would come after me, let him become more Christ-like." He said, "*If anyone would come after me, let*

---

[63] See the 144 page book, "The State of Discipleship" A Barna Report in Partnership with The Navigators, 2015
[64] The State of Discipleship, p 9
[65] The State of Discipleship, p 9

him deny himself and take up his cross daily and follow me. For whoever would save his life will lose it, but whoever loses his life for my sake will save it.'[66]

Only 1% of Church Leaders

According to the Barna/Navigators national study, "Only 1% (of Church leaders) say 'today's churches are doing very well at discipling new and young believers.'"[67] That is, only one out of a hundred leaders of churches in the USA think that today's churches are doing well in fulfilling the Great Commission of our Lord and Savior Jesus Christ among our youth! Since the goal of the Great Commission is *"make disciples of all nations."*

David Kinnaman, Barna's president, reminds us of the importance of his group's research on discipleship in the following bullet points:

- 84% of adults in the US, and 66% of practicing Christians, agree that 'the highest goal for life is to enjoy it as much as possible.'
- 91% of adults, and 76% of practicing Christians, believe that 'the best way to find yourself is to look inside yourself.'
- 97% of adults, and 91% of practicing Christians, agree that 'you have to be true to yourself.'[68]

When observing the data, he concluded, "People must not only convert to become a disciple of Jesus, but also de-convert from the religion of self."[69] I guess Kinnaman agrees with me that it is urgently important for American Christians in general to REPENT today!

So, instead of going through a meticulous accounting of the teaching of the New Testament on the 250+ times that the words: disciple, disciples and make disciples occur, which I have done in

---

[66] Luke 9:23-24
[67] The State of Discipleship, p10
[68] The State of Discipleship, p 14
[69] The State of Discipleship, p 15

other much longer books, I will briefly summarize here my conclusions made there.[70] I will share with you on the pages remaining, what I shared a couple weeks ago in Pakistan to the Christians I spoke with there.

A comprehensive reflection on what the New Testament and the teachings of Second Temple era rabbis[71] expressed on these terms of discipleship, have led me and others to conclude that they all agreed that there were **five marks** of a disciple. There is no doubt that Jesus added other specific requirements to these five general marks, all of which are very important.[72] But, for sake of the unanimous agreement of the meaning of "discipleship" in the NT era, we will focus only on the five marks. As you will quickly see, they are ample to prove the huge gap between NT disciples and most 21st century Christians.

1. Total Submission

Whenever someone followed a rabbi as a disciple, there was an understood relationship of complete devotion and subjection to the rabbi. By "total," I, of course, do not mean perfect submission. Plenty of mistakes and missteps would be made by the disciple. But there was no question that his[73] heart and attitude were all-in, nothing held back.

Matthew, a disciple who was elevated to the status of Apostle, carefully noted this requirement as stated by Jesus when He said, *"A disciple is not above his teacher, nor a servant above his master."*[74]

---

[70] See the two books: Are You a Christian or a Disciple? Rediscovering and Renewing NT Discipleship - Xulon Press, 2014 and Disciples Obey: How Christians Unknowingly Rebel against Jesus - Xulon Press, 2016

[71] Second Temple Judaism (2TJ) is generally the period from the rebuilt Temple (516 BC) to its destruction (70 AD). Some use 2TJ to refer more specifically to 168 BC – 70 AD.

[72] These extra elements of those who belonged to the School or Family of Jesus, His followers or disciples, may be deduced from the enduring commands He gave to them – see Appendix Two – Some of the Commands of Jesus

[73] Jesus is the only rabbi on record to have called women and children to be His disciples. He, no doubt, would have been often maligned for this. All other rabbis called only men (usually younger) to follow them.

[74] Matthew 10:24

The parallel in this verse should not be missed. A disciple is like a slave. A rabbi is like a slave's master.[75] Disciples submitted themselves to do what the rabbi commanded, immediately, and just as they were commanded to do it.

If it meant going somewhere undesirable, disciples went.[76] Or if they were told to do something, they did it as commanded by the rabbi, however implausible. Jesus shocked tired fishermen-becoming-disciples by commanding them, *"Put out into the deep and let down your nets for a catch. And Simon answered, 'Master, we toiled all night and took nothing! But at your word I will let down the nets.'"* What happened? *"And when they had done this, they enclosed a large number of fish, and their nets were breaking."*[77] Don't miss the total submission there!

Peter once was told how to pay taxes. Go fishing and take the money from the first fish caught and pay the temple tax![78] The Gospels are filled with such commands obeyed by the disciples of Jesus. But, how many churches are filled with such Christians?

The word "obey" is surely a four-letter word in most churches and to most westernized Christians today! But not to Pakistanis. And not to the hundreds of thousands of disciples arising from the DMMs all over the world.

Certainly, no 1st century disciple thought they could boldly disobey Rabbi Jesus. Yes, total submission was universally accepted as the cornerstone of the rabbi-disciple relationship. It was so honored that when a disciple followed a rabbi, the commands of the rabbi became more honored than those of the biological father! Rabbinic expert David Bivin wrote, "A special relationship developed between rabbi and disciple in which the rabbi became like

---

[75] The Greek terms for slave and master are not referring to the abhorrent system of the stealing, selling and breeding of human beings as existed in the United States from 1619-1863. It is referring in the NT era mainly to the relationship of someone who had sold himself into some form of slavery in order for the payment of a debt or to accrue assets needed by the slave, not legally available to him, otherwise.

[76] As in the story of going into Samaria in John 4

[77] Luke 5:4-6

[78] Matthew 17:27

a father. In fact, he was more than a father and was to be honored above the disciple's own father...."[79]

Maybe that is why Zebedee, when his sons dropped their nets and followed Jesus, was not noted as calling out to his sons, James and John, "Where are you going, boys? Don't you know this is our family business?" He knew what was happening. And the great honor it was to be chosen to follow a rabbi. Even at the cost of his own intimate relationship with his sons.

The Great Commission includes total submission as a key component, when Jesus said, "...*teach them to obey everything I have commanded you.*" Which of our teachers or pastors taught us that obedience to Jesus was a key component to the fulfilling of the Great Commission? It's right there in plain sight.

Imagine, this is just the first mark of a true disciple. How many Christians do you know who own it? Who love to subject their wills to the Lord's? Who have been well-discipled in obedience? How about you, yourself?

2. Total Mastery

The practice of NT era disciples was to memorize their rabbi's teaching perfectly. All of it. Verbatim. Jesus and other rabbis of the 1st century transmitted their teaching orally. No note taking. And how accurate was this form of communication? In fact,

> "The transmission of oral literature by rabbis and their disciples approached 100% accuracy, far greater than could have been achieved through written transmission.... The disciple of a sage was not permitted to alter even a word of a tradition he had received from his teacher when quoting him to others."[80]

---

[79] David Bivin, New Light on the Difficult Words of Jesus", p 19. Bivin heavily footnotes his material with rabbinic quotes from the Mishnah and Tosephta which recorded hundreds of years of the Oral Law of Judaism
[80] David Bivin, New Light, p34 and comments on m. Eduyot 1:3

Jesus expected His disciples to master His words. And He taught them that His words would become a most valuable and powerful force in their lives.

This is precisely what is behind His famous statement, *"If you abide in my word, you are truly my disciples, and you will know the truth, and the truth will set you free."*[81] Yet, as Christians, how deeply do we really value His Word? How many Bible College students or seminarians memorize more of God's Word than their lecturers' notes, which are soon forgotten after the test is taken?

Just consider three texts:

- *"What I tell you in the dark, say in the light, and what you hear whispered, proclaim on the housetops."*

- *"For whoever is ashamed of me and of my words in this adulterous and sinful generation, of him will the Son of Man also be ashamed when he comes in the glory of his Father with the holy angels."*

- *"But the Helper, the Holy Spirit, whom the Father will send in my name, he will teach you all things, and bring to your remembrance all that I have said to you."*[82]

Do you see how these verses demanded memorization by His disciples? Those early believers had no Bible, no buildings and no budget – yet they turned the world upside down! The words of Jesus filled their minds and guided their lives in the power of the Holy Spirit. What are we missing today?

This is why Paul, 20+ years later commanded the Colossians, *"Let the word of Christ dwell in you richly, teaching and admonishing one another in all wisdom...."*[83] The second mark leaves us in shock, as did the first. Something has got to change! It might be good to start confessing right now, before we move on to the third mark of a biblical disciple.

---

[81] John 8:31-32
[82] Matthew 10:27; Mark 8:38; John 14:26
[83] Colossians 3:16; See also Acts 20:35; 1 Timothy 6:3-4; 2 Timothy 1:13; 2 Peter 1:12-15; Revelation 2:26

Chapter Six

The Marks of a New Testament Disciple 2

It has simply left many Christian leaders reeling as they have been forced to evaluate their ministries by the simple question, "Have I made Christians or disciples of Jesus?" In our South African edition of Are YOU a Christian or a Disciple?, one of South Africa's leading theologians, Dr. Adrio Konig,[84] simply concluded, "One has to read this book to realize that we are merely creating Christians that have none of the characteristics of a disciple."[85] Having looked at the first 2 marks of a disciple, **total submission** and **total mastery**, let's move on prayerfully to the 3rd mark.

3. Total Understanding

D. Thomas Lancaster wrote,

> "In the days of the Master, the disciples of the sages (had this) major task to perform: To learn their teacher's traditions and interpretations. A disciple learned how his teacher kept the commands of God and interpreted the Scriptures. Every detail about the teacher was important ....
>
> To a disciple, these were like gems and pearls meant to be gathered and treasured."[86]

The most important section of the Gospels for discovering what Jesus believed about the Old Testament is the Sermon on the Mount. It's His mini-manual of discipleship. Many others have shown how His style in the first section paralleled the way rabbis

---

[84] Dr Konig served as Emeritus Professor at the Theological Faculty of UNISA – Pretoria, South Africa

[85] Are You a Christian or a Disciple, (SA edition – Sept 2014), back cover endorsement

[86] D Thomas Lancaster, King of the Jews, pp 52-53

would interact with or debate one another in those days. When Jesus said, "*You have heard it said, but I say to you,*"[87] He is comparing His interpretation and Way with those of other rabbis. It is, perhaps, just this that was being referred to in the book of Acts when the early Church was called the Way.[88]

The Way of a Rabbi

No disciple would follow a rabbi with whom he could not agree. And Jesus demanded an even stricter Way than the Pharisees, when He said, "*For I tell you, unless your righteousness exceeds that of the scribes and the Pharisees, you will never enter the kingdom of heaven.*"[89] His teachings on anger, lust, retaliation, love of enemies, etc. were, in His day, radical and remarkable. It left the crowds who heard Him, "*astonished at his teaching, for he was teaching them as one who had authority, and not as their scribes.*"[90]

But, His disciples were expected not only to be amazed. They were to adopt these teachings and live them out in real life. Turning the other cheek. Not laying up treasures on earth. Never worrying about the cares of this life. Doing to others what they would have them do to them. Few who first heard Him seemed to understand that He would fulfill the demands of the Law, Himself, in behalf of every disciple. And that His righteousness would be imputed to them by the Father, justifying them in His sight. The one indispensable work that must be done, which the disciples begged Him to tell them was revealed in these words: "*This is the work of God, that you believe in him whom he has sent.*"[91] And, little did they know that He would send the very Spirit of God, Himself, enabling and empowering them to walk in His Ways. True faith is never devoid of works, even when the works are not perfect.[92] Everything we are

---

[87] Matthew 5:21, 27, 31, 33, 38, 43
[88] See Acts 9:2; 19:9, 23; 22:4; 24:14, 42 and the helpful work of G.K. Beale, *New Testament Biblical Theology: The Unfolding of the Old Testament in the New*, pp. 856-858

[89] Matthew 5:20
[90] Matthew 7:28-29
[91] See John 6:28-29
[92] See Matthew 12:33-37; Hebrews 11; James 2:14-26; 1 John 3:16-18

and do needs to be "in Christ" in order to be acceptable to the Father.

How carefully, today, does a Christian consider the School of Jesus? How far we have truly fallen. How desperately we need His help. You see, to be a real part of His family, understanding and doing what He taught is not optional. For He, Himself said, *"Who are my mother and my brothers?... Here are my mother and my brothers! For whoever does the will of God, he is my brother and sister and mother."* [93]

No wonder that today in the USA there is such a discipleship dilemma! The cost is simply too great. There are too many Christian churches willing to cut deals in Jesus' name! You see, there will never be unity among Western Christians, because each group chooses what they want to include and exclude from the Way of Jesus. It, therefore, cannot surprise us why it is so hard to find agreement with the definition of a disciple.

A Fifth Gospel?

I want you to consider one man who squarely faced this dilemma and defeated it, with the help of the Spirit. His name was Pastor Juan Carlos Ortiz (1934-2021). A man who saw great struggles and successes in Buenos Aries, Argentina. What an autobiography of victory![94] Get his books and read them![95] I have devoured them. After he thoroughly studied and thought through the cost of discipleship as a pastor, he began to tell others that they could no longer pick and choose what they wanted to believe if they wanted to be a part of the church! He wrote,

> "Our modern gospel is what I call the Fifth Gospel. We have the gospels of Saints Matthew, Mark, Luke and John, and the Gospel according to Saint Evangelicals. The Gospel according to Saint Evangelicals is taken from verses here and there in the other four Gospels. We take all the verses we like, all the verses that offer something or promise

---

[93] Mark 3:33-34
[94] Juan C Ortiz, From the Jungles to the Cathedrals, 2011
[95] Disciple, 1975; Cry of the Human Heart, 1977; Living with Jesus Today, 1982, God is Closer than you Think, 1992

something—John 3:16; John 5:24, and so forth—and we make a systematic theology from these verses, while we forget the other verses that present the demands of Jesus Christ. Who authorized that? Who said we are allowed to present only one side of Jesus? ...
"I will give an example of the Fifth Gospel. Luke 12:32... But what about the next verse? "Sell your possessions and give to the needy." I've never heard a sermon on this verse, because it is not in the Gospel according to the Saint Evangelicals. Verse 32 is part of our Fifth Gospel, but verse 33 is not—and it is a command from Jesus. Who has the right to decide which commandments are compulsory and which are optional? You see, the Fifth Gospel has made a strange thing: an optional commandment! You do it if you want; if you don't, that's all right, too. But that's not the gospel of the Kingdom."[96]

They would have loved Pastor Ortiz in Pakistan! They weren't so excited when he came and taught Evangelical leaders in the USA!

4. Total Imitation

Jesus said, "*A disciple is not above his teacher; but everyone when he is fully trained will be like his teacher.*"[97] Today's Western form of education focuses on studying a subject and passing a test. Then moving on to the next subject and doing the same, until one graduates. That was not how rabbis made disciples. Yes, there were times of testing a disciple's competency. But, as Dr. Lancaster wrote,

"In Judaism, in the days of the apostles, the job of a disciple was well understood. A disciple's job was to become like his ... teacher.... At its simplest, discipleship is the art of imitation. It is the art of walking after a teacher."[98]

A Disciple is much more than a Student

---

[96] Juan C Ortiz, Disciple, pp 15, 17
[97] Luke 6:40
[98] Lancaster, King of the Jews, p 51

Discipleship was very different from today's general schooling. So, it really does a disservice when the word "disciple" is simply likened to a "student." Students do not expect to imitate their teacher's lifestyle. Disciples did.

How do most Western Christians approach their lifestyle? What influences them more: Jesus or the American Dream? Jesus was a homeless, wandering rabbi. When someone thought he was ready to join the School of Jesus as a disciple, He told him: *"Foxes have holes, and birds of the air have nests, but the Son of Man has nowhere to lay his head."*[99]

How did Jesus treat lepers, women, children, tax collectors and harlots? His disciples were expected to do the same. The topic Jesus most often addressed was that of money and property. How do most Christians in the USA approach money?

We are going to see that the way Jesus trained His disciples to trust Him as they would trust God, would go a long way in making them successful in their mission. Think of it, when Peter and John went to the temple to pray, they passed a man who had been lame all his life. He was begging for money. How did the disciples of Jesus handle the situation? Shockingly, to us!

> *"Peter said, 'I have no silver and gold, but what I do have I give to you. In the name of Jesus Christ of Nazareth, rise up and walk!"*[100]

But, this was no shock to the Spirit-empowered disciples. They simply did what they had seen their Rabbi do countless times before. They followed the behavior of Jesus.

Please, don't forget how the Church gave its offerings and gifts. They laid them *"at the feet of the apostles."*[101] Yes, those disciples of Jesus had plenty of money at their disposal. But, they did not stuff their pockets with it. Why? They were imitators of Jesus. There was one, though, who betrayed his discipleship. The Apostle who was *"the keeper of the money bag,"*[102] Judas Iscariot.

Yes, money matters to disciples because it mattered to Jesus. How we conduct ourselves in this world is often the real fruit that the Lord is looking for. How many Christians that you know, truly

---

[99] Luke 9:58
[100] Acts 3:6
[101] Acts 4:35,37; 5:2
[102] John 12:6 - NIV

live like Jesus? We don't because we don't have to. It's no longer expected. Why? Because we have substituted making disciples with making Christians and growing our churches.

5. Total Duplication

We have now reached the last of the five marks of a NT era disciple. And, yet again, we see a great chasm between it and the norm of Western Christianity. Today, most USA Christians expect our pastors, gifted Evangelists or attractive music ministries to be the main way of adding to our numbers. Maybe there are some bold congregations who have a Visitors Sunday once a month or so. But that every Christian is expected to spiritually reproduce and win others to Christ is hardly common. But, here is the challenging fact- - in the NT era, every disciple was expected to make disciples. No one was expected to be fruitless and barren in his/her witness.

That is why the Great Commission is for all of us. Jesus said it would stand *"to the end of the age."*[103] The Apostles are dead and we have not reached the end of the age. So, the Great Commission must not be only for them.

Jesus noted that the Pharisees had this goal in their discipling of others. *"You travel over land and sea to win a single convert...."*[104] All of Jesus' disciples expected that someday they would repeat the process and looked forward to doing that. The very first text in the Mishnah or Oral Torah passed on by rabbis to disciples throughout the ages of Judaism says this,

"Be patient in judgment. <u>Raise up many disciples</u>. Make a fence for the Torah."[105]

And wherever New Testament discipleship has been followed, this has been the practice. Every disciple learned how to reproduce and make disciples. Not so, today's Christianity!

---

[103] Matthew 28:20
[104] Matthew 23:15
[105] Mishnah Avot 1:1

What is Spiritual maturity?

Let's go back to Juan Carlos Ortiz and pick up a pivotal moment in his life as a young pastor. He remembered,

> "The Holy Spirit began to break me down. The first thing He said was, 'Juan, that thing you have is not a church. It's a business.'... Then the Lord told me a second thing. 'You are not growing,' He said. 'You think you are, because you've gone from 200 to 600. But you're not growing—you're just getting fat. All you have is more people of the same quality as before. No one is maturing; the level remains the same. Before you had 200 spiritual babies; now you have 600 spiritual babies....What you have is an orphanage instead of a church.'"[106]

The Lord then taught Pastor Ortiz to make disciples! He insisted that, just like in the physical world, we don't consider a child an adult until they pass through puberty. Until they can reproduce. So, it is in the Kingdom of Christ.

This is the same belief that is held in the Underground Church in China. The biography of Brother Yun, the Heavenly Man, is a story worth reading. But so is his book, Living Waters. In it, he declares,

> "Many Christians today are deceived. Somehow, they think that being saved means they can sit back and enjoy the Lord and do nothing else while they wait for Him to come again. This attitude is so strange to me that I find it astonishing. In China all the Christians I know are busy working for the Lord, preaching the gospel to people nearby and those far away.... In China every believer is an evangelist... Many Christians lead people to Jesus every single day. Some refuse to go to sleep until they have witnessed for the Lord and had the opportunity of bringing lost sheep into His fold."[107]

---

[106] Juan C Ortiz, Disciple, p 85
[107] Brother Yun, Living Water, p 232

They would love Brother Yun in Pakistan. He often speaks in our Western Evangelical churches today. And what does he do? He calls us to repentance. He noted,

> "You see, we are all called to run a race for Jesus, and repentance is the starting line of that race. It's futile to try to run the race if you have never made it to the starting line to begin with. This is the problem with many believers today. They are trying to follow the Lord, but they have never truly repented and surrendered their lives to Jesus Christ. The result of the false gospel so prevalent today can be seen in churches full of halfhearted Christians whose lives are still centered on selfishness and the principles of the world."[108]

So, to each large group I ministered to in Pakistan, I shared these 5 Marks of a NT disciple. And what was the response? In every single group there was weeping and repentance. These dear Christians were heart-struck by the obvious difference between being a Christian and being a disciple. So, when I called for a time of repentance, they responded with fervent confessions to God.

I would let this go on for a while, but then, remind them of the wonderful Gospel of Christ and the gift of forgiveness of sins— of the imputed righteousness that is ours by faith in Him. But, then I would move forward, as we are here, with the next subject: The Imperative of the Holy Spirit.

So, before, you read on about the empowering of God, take time to reflect and repent. Confessing that much of our Christianity today is devoid of the elements of NT Discipleship. Crying to the Father that we have far too often in the West chosen the easy and broad way of Christianity, a 5th Gospel, rather than embracing the whole counsel of God as a devoted disciple of Jesus. Please come alongside the Church in Pakistan as I saw it, with a broken spirit and contrite heart.

---

[108] Brother Yun, Living Water, p 18

Chapter Seven

The Imperative of the Holy Spirit

It's true - one of the great reasons why Disciple Making Movements (DMMs) are not arising in great numbers in the USA, is that there is little to no agreement in our churches as to what the word "disciple" means. But another, and to me a fatal error and omission in much of our Western disciple making efforts, is that we are far too often devoid of dependence on the person and work of the Holy Spirit of God. Too many of us think that we can fulfill the Great Commission without the daily, mighty work of the Holy Spirit as emphasized by Jesus in the very last words He spoke on earth. *"But you will receive power when the Holy Spirit has come upon you, and you will be my witnesses in Jerusalem and in all Judea and Samaria, and to the ends of the earth."*[109]

I long made that mistake. As a highly educated missiologist - with a high school diploma from a Christian high school, a bachelors degree (BA in Biblical Literature) from a Christian college, a Masters degree (MDiv) from a Christian seminary and a doctoral degree (DMis) from one of the most prestigious evangelical graduate institutions in the USA – I never was taught that the work of the Holy Spirit was indispensable for Christian ministry! That may come as a shock to some who read this. But, most American Evangelicals are undertaught on the necessity of the Holy Spirit in our ministries.

As I revealed in the Preface, I must admit, for all practical purposes, my Trinity had become: the Father, the Son and the Holy Scriptures! Pentecost did not really matter to me. Oh, theologically, I knew that the exalted Christ's pouring out of the Holy Spirit on His disciples[110] was significant. But, it is only now that I am beginning to fully appreciate that all of my progress as a disciple and of my Christian life and ministry would have been impossible without the Spirit's help. I love the translation that calls Him, "the

---

[109] Acts 1:8
[110] See Peter's declaration in his first Jerusalem message in Acts 2:33

Helper,"[111] because His help is much more than merely as a Comforter or Advocate, as precious as those are.

Jesus, Alone, is not enough

Was it really better for Jesus to leave so that the Spirit would come? Were the three+ years training of the Twelve by Christ, Himself really that deficient apart from His baptizing them with the Spirit on Pentecost? Is it really right to regard the Spirit, in some ways, as Jesus' divine Successor on earth? Does the Holy Spirit really "teach us all things"? Is His work so vital that the Apostle John would declare, *"But the anointing that you received from him abides in you, and you have no need that anyone should teach you. But as his anointing teaches you about everything, and is true, and is no lie – just as it has taught you, abide in him"*?[112]

For the vast amount of my Christian ministry (ordained in 1978), I would have answered these questions as NO, when the answer is YES. It was not until I took a month and totally devoted myself to studying what the Bible says about the Spirit's person and work, that I realized how deficient my biblical education had been! Please read Appendix Three at the end of this book to see some of the fruit of what I discovered from the nearly 300 times the Spirit is mentioned in the New Testament.[113] Jesus clearly taught that He, alone was not enough. We must have the Spirit that He poured out!

A Person, not a Force

We, together with all Christians through the New Testament, are seriously warned about lying to, resisting, grieving, quenching and outraging the Holy Spirit.[114] Rather, we are commanded to be baptized with, empowered by, led by, constantly

---

[111] The ESV in John 14-16
[112] 1 John 2:27
[113] Appendix Three – A Summary of the Person and Work of the Holy Spirit
[114] Acts 5:3-4; 7:51; Ephesians 4:30; 1 Thessalonians 5:19; Hebrews 10:29

filled with, to live by, keep in step with, and to pray in the Holy Spirit![115]

When I consider that the blessed Spirit of God is a divine PERSON, sent to abide in my body as His temple, and not merely as a force or extension of God in some impersonal way – I truly shudder. For how many years did I virtually disregard His personal presence and work in and around me! I often ignored Him. I refused to pray to Him. So, I hardly worshipped Him. And never with my whole heart!

How many of us, because of a theological position, disregard the One who is called the Gift, the Promise and the very "Power from on high?"[116] I was so proud and foolish in this regard. But God gave me grace, hearing my repentance and filling me afresh with His presence, power and love. And He allowed me to bathe in the memorization and meditation of the whole of Scriptures afresh, as the very words of the Holy Spirit of God.

I cherish now my "fellowship" with the Holy Spirit more than I do with that of any human being.[117] As I am thrust by the Lord of the harvest into the harvest every day, it is principally the work of precious Spirit of God within me that guides me to His prepared people of peace who await my discipling!

"The Full Gospel"

I now believe that each of those Evangelical traditions which suppresses the Holy Spirit also suppresses the full blessing of the gospel of Jesus Christ. With Paul, I am determined, "when I come to you, I will come in the fullness of the gospel of Christ."[118] I can hardly speak of the levels we teachers and preachers need to repent in reference to our grieving the Holy Spirit in what we have withheld from so many Christians in the USA. No wonder we are seeing almost NO Disciple Making Movements when the rest of the world is enjoying the blessing of nearly 2000 DMMs flourishing in

---

[115] Acts 1:5; 1:8; Romans 8:14; Ephesians 5:18; Galatians 5:25; Jude 20
[116] See Luke 1:35; Acts 2:38; 8:20; 10:45; 11:17; Luke 24:49; Acts 1:8
[117] See 2 Corinthians 13:14
[118] Romans 15:29

their midst, reviving their lives, saving their souls and transforming their cultures.[119]

And, it should be clearly noted that, churches from Pentecostal and Charismatic backgrounds need to realize that they have not birthed DMMs in the USA, either. So, it is obviously possible to think highly of the Holy Spirit and, yet, to grieve His true Great Commission work of making disciples. How? By being deceived by sin or Satan in other ways like pride, division, advancing counterfeits, etc. The contemporary works of Reformed/charismatic Dr. RT Kendall and Dr. Michael Brown are especially helpful in warning "Spirit-filled brethren" in this regard.[120]

Pakistan – Spiritually Ready

You could hardly imagine the thrill in my heart when I began questioning Saqib about working together in Pakistan. I had to know if the work of the Spirit was vital to him and his ministry. He immediately and wholeheartedly affirmed that he was a man surrendered to the Holy Spirit and that those churches and leaders laboring with him in Christ for All Nations (Pakistan) were all men and women who adored and strove to be filled with the Holy Spirit!

The USA – Terribly Divided

I used to not like the phrase, "baptized with the Spirit." Until I discovered that I was opposing one of the great works of Jesus Christ, exalted in Glory as King of all kings. For it was John who declared, *"I baptize you with water ... but he who is coming after me is mightier than I .... He will baptize you with the Holy Spirit and with fire."*[121]

---

[119] See the testimonies in books like Miraculous Movements (Trousdale); Father Glorified (Robertson); A Wind in the House of Islam (Garrison); Contagious Disciple Making (Dave and Paul Watson); Mission Frontiers magazine

[120] See, for instance, RT Kendall's Holy Fire: A Balanced, Biblical Look at the Holy Spirit's work in our lives; Pigeon Religion: Holy Spirit, is that you? Discerning Spiritual Manipulation; Word & Spirit; Michael Brown's Revival or We Die; Playing with Holy Fire: a Wake-up Call to the Pentecostal-Charismatic Church

[121] Matthew 3:11

Who does the baptizing with the Holy Spirit? Jesus! Did that surprise Him, because He baptized no one with the Holy Spirit during His earthly ministry? No, because in Acts, *"after he had given commands through the Holy Spirit to the apostles whom he had chosen .... And while staying with them he ordered them not to depart from Jerusalem, but to wait for the promise of the Father, which, he said, 'you heard from me; for John baptized with water, but you will be baptized with the Holy Spirit not many days from now.'"*[122]

Jesus knew His time to baptize with the Spirit was about to happen. So, Peter, on the Day of Pentecost with all the others in the house received the baptism and *"they were all filled with the Holy Spirit and began to speak in tongues as the Spirit gave them utterance."*[123] Note, that the baptism is also called a filling. Later, Peter declared in his first message, used powerfully by the Spirit to save 3000 men, plus untold numbers of women and children:

> *"This Jesus, delivered up according to the definite plan and foreknowledge of God, you crucified and killed by the hands of lawless men. God raised him up, loosing the pangs of death, because it was not possible for him to be held by it.... This Jesus God raised up, and of that we are all witnesses. BEING THEREFORE EXALTED AT THE RIGHT HAND OF GOD, AND HAVING RECEIVED FROM THE FATHER THE PROMISE OF THE HOLY SPIRIT, HE HAS POURED OUT THAT THIS YOU YOURSELVES ARE SEEING AND HEARING."*[124]

And every single time that the "baptism," the "filling," the "coming upon" of the Spirit happens in Acts, the joyous recipients do one thing – they SPEAK. Not always, or even usually, in an unknown language. But they cannot help but share the good news powerfully with others. Jesus had predicted this – *"But you will receive power when the Holy Spirit has come upon you, and you will be my witnesses...*

---

[122] Acts 1:2-5
[123] Acts 2:1-4
[124] Acts 2:23-24, 32-33

to the end of the earth."[125] Do the thorough study for yourselves and you will see that it is true. When we are filled with the Spirit, we must open our mouths and share with others the glorious Word of God![126] There is no such thing as a silence-produced filling of the Holy Spirit.

Believe and Receive

So, I say to you, wherever you may be living, *"Repent, and be baptized every one of you in the name of the Lord Jesus Christ for the forgiveness of your sins, and you will receive the gift of the Holy Spirit. For the promise is for you and for your children, and for all who are far off, everyone whom the Lord our God calls to himself."*[127] The Spirit of God is your rightful inheritance! Just as you received Jesus by faith, receive the Holy Spirit by an act of faith! A passive approach to Jesus leaves a person unsaved. A passive approach to the Spirit leaves a person without His greatest inward influences.

Many years later, when John wrote His gospel of Jesus, he couldn't help remembering those glorious days:

"On the last day of the feast, the great day, Jesus stood up and cried out, 'If anyone thirsts, let him come to me, as the Scripture has said, 'Out of his heart will flow rivers of living water.''" Now this he said about the Spirit, whom those who believed in him were to receive, for as yet the Spirit had not been given, because Jesus was not yet glorified."[128]

You may have already believed and received Jesus. Well, believe and receive the Spirit's empowering presence for your empowered, courageous witness. By faith, receive Him in an Acts 1:8 way. For super focus, wisdom and power to speak of Christ. *"If you, then, who*

---

125 Acts 1:8
126 See all 9 instances in (1) Acts 2:4,11, 16-17; (2) 4:8; (3) 4:23-31; (4) 6:3,5,7, 10; (5) 9:17,20; (6) 10:44-48; (7) 11:22-24; (8) 13:9-10; (9) 19:6 – and compare Acts 4:29-30; 5:18-19; 2 Tim 1:7-8 and Rev 22:17
127 Acts 2:38-39
128 John 7:37-39

are evil, know how to give good gifts to your children, how much more will the heavenly Father give the Holy Spirit to those who ask!" [129]

And how they asked in Pakistan! No, they didn't simply ask, they cried out, some standing with outstretched arms, others abased bowing their faces to the earth. I can see them by the hundreds — renewed by the grace and Spirit of God. And once, they repented and cried to be filled — I knew I could move forward with the truths that would fill them with such hope and rejoicing! That is what is ahead of you, too. But, do not rush to the next chapter. Receive your filling now by asking and you will see the waters flow from you as never before! Because you will soon be making disciples of many around you in Acts 1:8 power!

---

[129] Luke 11:13

Part Three
Discipleship – How?

Chapter Eight

Obey and Pray
Luke 10:1-2

The passage we will focus on for the rest of this little book is Luke 10:1-12 (10:1-23 in its entire context). This has been called Jesus' strategy for world missions that has been "hidden in plain sight." How much of the Word has been virtually locked away from us because we have lived a "pick and choose" approach to the Word, like Ortiz called it – the Gospel of Saint Evangelicals? Let's turn from any short-cut approach and remember what Jesus declared to Satan when first tempted in the wilderness, *"Man shall not live by bread alone, but by every word that comes from the mouth of God."*[130] Let your mission be Word-driven!

Read like a Disciple Heard

"Take care then how you hear, for to the one who has, more will be given, and from the one who has not, even what he thinks that he has will be taken away." [131] If you are given grace to read these words, like little children, not trying to figure everything out, but OBEYING the Word, then – you will surely be blessed! How you hear is crucial. Are you primarily an analyst, or primarily a believer, and doer of the Word? Yes, we can and should do both. But, beware, few are doing both well. Somewhere between the text and the conclusions we make, too often the Spirit is lost, and the drive to obey is set aside.

As you begin this section, I wish I could transport you to Pakistan so that you could witness what these verses did for the souls of Christians there. These verses were like wood that the Spirit of God, the fire of God, would ignite into a great fire in their lives. I beheld a spiritual resurrection happening in every place that I shared these verses. Hope, comfort, boldness, desire and determination

---

[130] Matthew 4:4 quoting Deuteronomy
[131] Luke 8:18

were set aflame by these truths in the hearts of today's persecuted minority of Pakistan. May they, by the power of the Holy Spirit, have the same impact on you, wherever you may be, in cultures of opposition or openness. In lands marked by repression or freedom.

"After this the Lord appointed seventy-two others"

Luke 10 happened late in the ministry of Jesus. It was about a year later than when He had sent out the 12 on their short-term mission trip.[132] The 70 (rounded down) or 72 were "seventy-two others," that is they were other than the apostles. That is WHY this text is so pivotal for us in the post-apostolic era. We are not apostles.[133] But we are disciples. And, therefore, more like the 72 than like the 12. And, remember, the Great Commission, though given to the apostles, was not only for them – because "the end of the age" is yet ahead of US. Luke 10 happened when there was only about six months left before the crucifixion.

What a treasure is THIS account! We would not have known that there were many who Jesus trained, and were ready to go, other than the apostles, if it were not for this text and a few divine snippets elsewhere. Lord, help us to gather up these "fragments" of revelation from Your precious Word, so that nothing will be lost.

"sent them on ahead of him…into every town and place where he himself was about to go"

This teaches us that Jesus, by the Spirit, knew where He would be going in the future. And the Jesus that we, today, are "following" is not the earth-bound Son of Man; but the heaven-enthroned King of kings! We follow the One to whom has been

---

132 See Matthew 10:5-15; Mark 6:7-13; Luke 9:1-6
133 The NT reveals the various elements of what Paul called, "the marks of an apostle," (what has been called "apostolocity") and the Ephesian church knew how to "test those who call themselves apostles and are not" (Revelation 2:2). So, we need to be very wary of self-termed apostles and simply, humbly follow Jesus, letting the Spirit distribute the gifts "to each one individually as he wills" (1 Corinthians 12:11).

given "*all authority in heaven and on earth.*"[134] By "*every town and place,*" we must be ready to apply from this passage its truths wherever we go. The context focuses on specific towns they would visit and live in for a while; but, the application is for every **place** as well. This does not relate, today, only to missionaries leaving their culture. It relates to wherever we as disciples go. To McDonalds, Walmart, to school or to a park. That is why disciples TODAY are fruitfully following this revelation wherever we go.

Lord, Jesus, You are alive and reigning today, right now! Please send us mainly to those places and people where You have gone before us, doing a work of preparation. May we realize that You desire to guide our every step into every place we travel. Help us, everywhere, to be on mission.

"two by two"

Partnering was and is His plan. But, this does not mean that everywhere we go, we go only with a partner. The disciples did things individually. But, in the process of discipling receptive hearers, near or far, partnering is best whenever possible. Why? Because there is safety in numbers. One can only see and be aware of so much. If we really are at war, then we are in danger. Enemies are less likely to attack two than one. And Satan is less likely of distracting and detouring two than one. So, there is also wisdom in numbers, rather than in solitude. We give up much quicker when alone. And we fall into sin much more readily when alone, than when we are with a fellow-disciple.

But, to me, the main reason to add what Paul called "a true companion,"[135] is that there is special spiritual power in prayer when there are "*two of you who agree on earth about anything they ask.*"[136] Jesus promised, "*For where two or three are gathered in my name, there am I among them.*"[137] The whole success of our mission, as we will see, depends on prayer. It is a beautiful thing wherever brethren dwell together in

---

[134] Matthew 28:18
[135] See Philippians 4:3; 2:25; Colossians 1:7
[136] Matthew 18:18
[137] Matthew 18:20

the spirit of unified prayer. It is a powerful, Kingdom advancing thing!

Lord, please give me someone with whom I can share the burdens and blessings of this mission of making disciples. And may I always be preparing younger disciples by taking them with me into the whitened, harvest-ready fields. And, for all of us who are blessed by marriage, please give us, with our spouses, a life of unhindered, powerful, united prayer.[138]

The Harvest Prayer of Jesus – 10:2

"The harvest is plentiful, but the laborers are few. Therefore, pray earnestly to the Lord of the harvest to send out laborers into his harvest."

Here, before sending out the 72, and previously, when sending out the 12 apostles,[139] Jesus commanded His disciples to pray these exact words. I daily pray the Lord's Prayer, as do many Christians globally. And that prayer was also given twice, though not in the same form.[140] Why do we pray the Lord's Prayer and do not pray the Harvest Prayer?[141] It is not prayer in general that should precede our work of outreach, it is the exact words and specific petitions of this prayer. Remember, disciples did what their Rabbi commanded. They would have memorized and prayed these very words – with faith. So should we, for we are disciples, also.

"The harvest is plentiful"

The harvest is souls who are going to be saved. People who are being readied to be saved. Not the world in general; but the chosen in particular.[142] We are here reminded that there are many

---

138 See 1 Peter 3:7

139 See Matthew 9:35-38

140 See Matthew 6:9-13 and Luke 11:2-4

141 See my book, The Harvest Prayer of Jesus: *Why American Christians are Missing Today's Global Renewal*

142 The Scriptures refers to these "chosen" by many terms like the sheep, those whom you have given me out of the world, the wheat, the good soil, the elect, the

who will be saved. A great harvest is not just a few plants. The Revelation describes the number and diversity of the people of God in these words: *"a great multitude that no one could number, from every nation, from all tribes and peoples and languages, standing before the Lamb...."*[143] Why did Jesus want to remind them and us of this truth? Because it is possible that we are near or in the harvest without even knowing it. Largely, perhaps, as the people He is getting ready to save may not look like us or speak our language. They could very well be people we would not choose to associate with or feel a love for. Just be aware of this – if the Lord is now getting your attention to increase your witness, you should expect fruitfulness. But, be ready, the harvest may bring total strangers to you, with strange customs you are not used to. They will specially appreciate your attempts to learn new things through them.

"but the laborers are few"

By revealing this fact, Jesus reveals that there is a general crisis around each willing soulwinner. That there is a big harvest, but few workers. Many to be saved, but few who are skilled in helping them into the Kingdom. So, how is Jesus going to solve this manpower problem? By commanding the workers to work overtime? By adding pressure? By saying that Herculean strength will be needed to bring in the harvest? You may be surprised – but the resounding answer is, NO! God does not need you to work harder, but to work smarter. And that is the KEY. We must understand the miracle of God in using us to gather the harvest. It is by a divinely-appointed peace, not by a humanly-produced pressure.

"Therefore, pray earnestly to the Lord of the harvest"

Think of it, Jesus has a solution for this manpower problem! That's what *"therefore"* addresses and remedies. Yes, God knows who

---

Bride of Christ, the foreknown, the predestined, etc. By these terms we are forever humbled and remember that salvation is truly by grace, not by works, so that no one can boast (Ephesians 2:8-9).
143 Revelation 7:9

will be saved, together with when and where they will be saved. Jesus, ever so graciously, commands us to call God, *"the Lord of the harvest"* when we pray to Him concerning the mission. He has the harvest under His sovereign control and wants to bring us into the blessing of His divine knowledge and plan. God has many names. Jesus here focuses on just one, when we pray concerning the lost around us. And that is because He wants us to know that God always has the salvation of others in His heart. So, whenever we are burdened for the souls of others, we can know that God is, too. But calling on God rightly does not mean only using the right phrase, Lord of the harvest.

Jesus commands us to be earnest about it. To pray fervently. To rightly consider the enormity of that for which we are praying. How moved we should be with the condition and plight of the lost, as we pray for them. They are dangling by a thread over the fires of hell. They are in danger of standing before a holy and righteous Judge totally unprepared. They are all in imminent danger of which few have any idea or worry! They are blind and do not know their perilous state. They are proud and do not realize it. They are already condemned and just awaiting the execution of their horrible sentence. For *"whoever does not obey the Son shall not see life, but the wrath of God remains on him."*[144]

Please, with me, cast off passivity, doubt and ambivalence as we pray for the lost. And for all the lost – for the whole harvest wherever it may be. Let's not just cry tears for our lost kids or those we know. But for everyone. It is only then that we will share the compassion that gripped our Savior when He looked around Him and *"had compassion for them, because they were harassed and helpless, like sheep without a shepherd."*[145] The same heart of sadness that gripped Him when He first gave the Harvest Prayer to the apostles and the 72, should grip us as we pray it! Help us, Holy Spirit!

---

[144] John 3:36
[145] Matthew 9:36

"to send out laborers into his harvest"

As we pray, we are asking for something very specific. For a miracle. That the Lord of the harvest would not let a single disciple maker waste his time by laboring outside of the harvest, on hard soil and rejecting hearts. Oh yes, we will scatter seed; but, we are not to labor there, as we will see. He has told us where to labor – in the harvest.

We need a word, too, about what a harvest "laborer" looks like. They can look like only one thing – devoted, both hands-on-the-plow disciples! Like hard-working servants, because disciple making is not easy work. It's much more labor intensive than merely riding into a place and declaring a message, even the gospel. The work is in praying. The work is in denying and preparing oneself as a disciple maker, discovering what tools are best being used in each harvest. We must prayerfully and practically ascertain which works of love will open the most doors. And engage in those works purposefully: to win confidence as real Christ followers, filled with selfless love. We do not punch a time clock as disciples. All of this, and more, is meant by the Lord directing us to pray for real laborers. How can one be considered as a laborer for foreign fields, if he/she has not labored hard in following Jesus fruitfully right where he/she may be?

Wherever DMMs have occurred, great devotion to prayer has preceded. All that this is saying is: God is a personal God and will not advance the Kingdom in an automatic, impersonal way. There must be communication between Him and us. Do you love to talk with God? Many Christians don't. Some are afraid of what He may say or demand of them. Others act like God must speak only Hebrew or Greek, which they do not know. Like, God doesn't speak our language. Still others don't like to wait on God. Silence is awkward to many. But, it's worth the wait. And God is not usually gabby. There may only be a few words by a "still small voice." Oh, how little do we bathe in His unchanging, ever-flowing love for us! Even when evangelism and missions is in mind.

We can easily forget that behind everything happening in this world is, *"For God so loved the world."*[146] Our Harvest Prayer times should be the greatest times of receiving and expressing the language of love. I have seen it universally. Prayer meetings for the fulfillment of the Great Commission (following Luke 10), are the greatest meetings where expressions of love are shared and experienced.

What hope do Christians have that the Lord will use them "in the harvest" if they do not even know what a disciple is? Likewise, how will a God who is love use us if our communication with Him in prayer is purely tactical and rarely emotional? So, we must till the soil of Christianity again until the marks of a true disciple are commonly known and aspired for. And, as this chapter reveals, until we love to speak with and receive from Jesus the assurance of His abiding presence with us wherever we go in His Name.

---

[146] John 3:16

Chapter Nine

GO

Luke 10:3-4

After we pray, we are to go. Here is where many well-intentioned witnesses get sidetracked. By unnecessary waiting or hesitating. We are strong in prayer and then sheepish to go. You see, we often exercise our spirits when we pray. And that is us at our best – when we are spiritually guided and empowered. But, after the prayer, all too often, we shift from living in the presence of God, back down to being mainly earthly-minded. We shift from being spiritually minded to being carnally minded.[147] The best time "to go" is directly after praying. Or to stay continually in prayer, wherever you go.[148] So, Jesus now continues His brilliant, winning pattern of missions.

> **"Go your way; behold, I am sending you out**
> **as lambs in the midst of wolves."**

We must go prayerfully. But where? We are to go "our way." That is, to the place where the Lord has led us to go. It varies person-to-person. And, unless we are on a mission, like the 72, it will be different from day-to-day. It is wonderful to see how the Spirit of the Lord will lead a group of disciples directly into a harvest situation after gathering and praying for guidance for a short time! This is happening globally – even in the USA.

The word translated, "*behold*" means something like – "take special note of this." My dear Pakistani brothers and sisters did just that – and it filled them with awe and encouragement. When I reminded them that our God of sovereign power is also a God of tender love, carefully watching over His Flock and carrying His little lambs in His arms – they wept with joy! Yes, Jesus cares for us when

---

147 See Romans 8:5-8; Galatians 5:16-17
148 1 Thessalonians 5:17

we are surrounded by threatening opponents who, like Saul of Tarsus, are *"breathing threats and murder against the disciples of the Lord."*[149]

Jesus knows that the circumstances into which He sends us, out of love for the lost, are often perilous. But He still sends us. Yet, as we will soon see, not ever to risk our lives unnecessarily. No, He loves us far too much to do that. *"If you then, who are evil know how to give good gifts to your children, how much more will your Father who is in heaven give good things to those who ask Him!"*[150]

I cannot rightly relate how dearly and deeply that touched the hearts of my dear Pakistani hearers. But, it certainly prepared them for the good news that Jesus can use us in fulfilling the Great Commission without everywhere, everyday fearing death. They felt "at home" with me, as a brother and as a father, because I let Jesus assure them of His love – with tears.

There is still one verse, with some important ground rules, that we must consider before we get to the miracle promise and provision that God made to all of us disciples who go in Jesus' name.

"Carry no moneybag"

How does this specific command apply to us today? First, by teaching us that money really does not matter most in the fulfillment of the Great Commission. Jesus will provide if the disciple follows His instructions. He always has and always will. So, all the hype of great financial campaigns that sometimes last for years, without leading to true disciple making, may be, in the end, a great waste of time, money, talents and lives.

There is no greater weakness and selfishness revealed in our Western mission endeavor than the coveting of money. Paul warns of this as idolatry[151]. And the jealous guarding of one's donor list may reveal it, too! The love of money is a Christ-denying characteristic, whether it be by an individual or by a mission agency. Jesus trained His apostles and disciples for years on this principle and, at the end, wanted to make sure that they did not miss the point.

---

149 Acts 9:1
150 Matthew 7:11
151 See Colossians 3:5

Jesus loved and will ever love them, providing for their needs – if they will just believe and obey.

On the night He was betrayed, listen to how Jesus sent this point home to their hearts. *"And he said to them, 'When I sent you out with no moneybag or knapsack or sandals, did you lack anything?' They said,* **'Nothing.'"** What? Faith and obedience, trusting the Lord to provide, is actually enough? How many American mission agencies have trained their missionaries in this truth? And how many trust it for the running of the agency, itself? Often, today, the missionary believes, but the agency does not.

"no knapsack, no sandals, and greet no one on the road"

But, we will die of exposure during the cold nights. Our feet will get torn up by worn-out footwear. We will look like unfriendly, uncouth, disheveled vagabonds. What would we have thought had these words been spoken to us? By the way, when Jesus sent the 72 out, the weather was getting colder. These commands forced the disciples to test the faithfulness of the Lord. Some could have thought of this very negatively. Lord, we are not prepared to go. We are undersupplied. But they did not say it because they had learned that Jesus was a kindhearted, miracle worker. That He knew what He was talking about. They had learned that they could really trust Him. Have we?

When He said, *"don't greet,"* it was to keep them from getting sidetracked. From trying to cut a deal or manipulate someone into helping them. Like we would have done. That command was saying, "You are on My mission. Stay focused or you may never even arrive, much less fulfill the mission." The devil has many ways to discourage and detour the Christian. It doesn't take much. But, not with the disciple who obeys His Master's commands – and doesn't take them to be merely helpful hints.

So, while the 72 were, perhaps, reeling from the shockingly barebones approach of Jesus, they could easily have missed His remedy. Perhaps we would have, looking around and rolling our eyes. Thankfully, those early disciples did not. Rather, they heard of the miraculous strategy that would solve all their food, clothing, sleeping and housing needs, because all 72 actually went. Even after these rules for going were given.

When the Pakistani Christians heard this passage, just weeks ago, they were encouraged. Are you? Many Americans are not, because they are Christians not disciples. We are used to comfort and ease. And can start complaining very quickly. Consider this, that nowhere do we see Jesus or any of His disciples traveling by any mode but by foot, except for the Triumphal Entry of Jesus into Jerusalem on our Palm Sunday. They walked everywhere. And in sandals, not in Nikes or Adidas. For years, over all types of rocky and dusty terrain, and in all types of weather. For many Christians today, that, alone, would be intolerably tough, demanding too much sacrifice. We've grown soft and discipleship does not know soft.

Dear Father, prepare our hearts to go as Jesus taught us to go. In selfless love. And bless your children everywhere, in poverty or in riches, with the grace to follow Jesus and make many disciples despite their conditions. Please help us to believe in the power of prayer. And to depend on You, embracing prayer as a first practice, rather than as a last, desperate resort. Help us to believe in the miraculous way that Jesus said He would provide for and use His disciples to save others, as the 72 did – and as so many experiencing DMMs today are finding to be true. Lord, I believe. Help my unbelief!

Chapter Ten

Find and Disciple

Luke 10:5-7

Examining **these** verses became the moment of truth to my Pakistani audiences. It was with what Jesus now said that everything turned. If they believed it and started doing it – they would experience a new day of unparalleled blessing. If they refused to believe and obey, they would drift back into the old life of fear and relative fruitlessness. The same is true for you. So, pray that the Spirit will give you *"eyes to see and ears to hear."* Otherwise, you, too will hesitate, in deadly disbelief and disobedience, and drift back to the old Christian ways. I am praying that each of you will believe, grab hold and be thrust forward into the harvest of souls, making disciples who never stop making disciples until Jesus returns.

"Whatever house you enter, first say, 'Peace to this house!'"

We have seen that the NT era disciples did what their rabbis told them to do. This was true of the disciples of Jesus, too. It is true of disciples of Christ today as well. And when the Master says to do something *"first,"* you do not make it second. Or last. Or forget it altogether. It is first for a reason, whether we appreciate its significance or not. We are to obey like little children.

Speaking "peace" as our first step into a house, or into whatever setting you are entering, is a step of faith. And it is significantly powerful as a first-step of finding the people who have been prepared by the Spirit to be discipled. Think of how easy it is to do this! Prayerfully whispering four words will often prove the success or failure of a mission endeavor. Because it is for the faith-filled utterance of those words that the Triune God is waiting to hear! *"Faith to this place."*

What a combination of the natural and the supernatural occurs when the believing disciple enters a place with those words. It is natural, because it is we who are praying them. And it is supernatural because God works wonders in response to them. I have seen it happen scores of times. Before entering a home, McDonalds, Dunkin Donuts, an airplane, a hotel, a church building, a store, a park, a group of people standing in a soup line, etc. I have seen God open amazing and fruitful doors of evangelism and disciple making **just from speaking those words by faith in Jesus' name** (that is, believing in His presence with me). And I have heard and read of the same thing happening countless thousands of times by disciples across the world.

Because this book is simulating my messages in Pakistan, I will refrain from multiplying its pages by sharing many of the stories I could share. We did not have to share the stories in Pakistan – because the disciples there believed the Word, itself! And because we did not have time. I love to share those testimonies.[152]

If you, the reader, will determine to follow Jesus in this first step, you will be well on your way to seeing God work mightily through you, producing 30, 60 or 100-fold of disciples! But, the question is, are you "good soil?" Are you receptive to the Word? Will you follow Jesus in literal obedience?[153]

The whole Luke 10 strategy of Jesus is absurd to our rational minds. It is impossible! But ours is the God of the impossible, as the angel Gabriel reminded Mary, *"for nothing will be impossible with God."*[154] Perhaps the implausible reality of such great outcomes as Disciple Making Movements (DMMs) resulting from such simple steps as the Harvest Prayer and then, speaking peace to a place is why it has taken missionaries so long to return to Luke 10 as their strategy. It seems "too good to be true." And when facing something like that, we have always been taught to be cautious and get ready to run! But, doesn't

---

[152] We are now preparing a 2nd volume, just of testimonies, to thrill our readers with God's power and faithfulness to do just as He has promised to do. Read Jerry Trousdale's, *Miraculous Movements: How Hundreds of Thousands of Muslims are Falling in Love with Jesus* to see how the Lord prepared 18,000+ people of peace to receive disciples following Luke 10, who ultimately made 100,000+ new disciples of Jesus across Sub-Saharan Africa in less than 10 years!

[153] See Matthew 13:1-9 and its interpretation by Jesus in 13:18-23. It will sober you considerably reading what Jesus said, too, in 13:10-17!

[154] Luke 1:37

it make sense that a God who loves the entire world would also make it clear and simple how to reach them?

Our strategies for reaching the world have seemed so much more likely to succeed to us because, well, they are *our* best ideas. How little have we realized why hundreds of years of missionary efforts have produced so little fruit. It has not been because missionaries and churches haven't been prayerful and sacrificial. Or sincere and self-denying. It is, perhaps, because we haven't carefully followed Jesus' way of praying and going. Much has been accomplished. But, how much more could have been done had we and our brave predecessors known Luke 10 and followed it. We thank God that is all changing in our day.

"And if a son of peace is there, your peace will rest upon him. But if not, it will return to you."

This verse, and its divine promise, is the miracle of God's grace. How does a believer best fulfill the Great Commission in a persecuting environment where they are going forth as lambs amid wolves? Or in a friendlier context where there is no or little threat to their lives? By always going and following the plan of Jesus.

We go with peace not pressure. Our approach is not primarily to win someone over by argument. It is to find the right person at the right place at the right time. The "person of peace" whom the Lord has been working in and bringing them to a harvestable condition. Pastor Saqib and I both knew of the brilliant Pakistani apologist, Dr. K. L. Nasir, who is reported on his deathbed to have said, "I have won so many debates, but so few to Christ." Sometimes well-framed arguments have proven helpful in nudging people to faith. But that is not how DMMs are being birthed today.

So, when we come into contact with a person, what are we looking for? What characteristic will mark them as a likely person of peace? It is one chief quality – they are **receptive**. They are drawn to us. They are willing and able to help us. They are unusually ready. This is the promise of God.

That also explains why the 72 did not need to take bedding with them. The Lord had already made their beds for them by supernaturally going before them and creating an atmosphere of hospitality for them.

If someone is cold and irresponsive, don't push it. Your *"peace has returned"* back to you, and has been rejected by the person. Don't complain. Move on. The person might respond in the future to someone else. But now isn't their time.

This is a rather simple strategy, isn't it? Notice how the risk has been largely taken away. You have smiled and been friendly. And so have they. Things have clicked and you feel that special vibe of affinity with the person. They aren't itching to get away. Their body language isn't shouting, "I'd rather be somewhere else. I don't have time for you." Rather, they seem comfortable. Perhaps even strangely comfortable with you. It is "a God moment" for sure. That's the most effective evangelism – by peace not pressure.

> **"And remain in the same house, eating and drinking what they provide, for the laborer deserves his wages."**

The 72 were assured of safety if they traveled down this path. They would know when they had landed into a harbor of peace. Their food and board were supernaturally provided for in a very natural way. And Jesus wanted them to know that He saw what they were doing as real work, worthy of real reward. Earlier, in Samaria, Jesus had similarly taught the 12, *"Look I tell you, lift up your eyes, and see that the fields are white for harvest. Already the one who reaps is receiving wages and gathering fruit for eternal life...."*[155] What an amazing God we serve! All we mainly do is show up and speak peace, while exuding a spirit of peace and love, by His grace. And He does the rest!

Why should we be surprised? Isn't He the God of salvation? Isn't He *"patient ... not wishing that any should perish, but that all should reach repentance."*?[156] Hasn't He always done all the heavy lifting regarding our salvation? Doesn't this look just like what Jesus said,

---

[155] John 4:35-36
[156] 2 Peter 3:9

No one can come to me unless the Father who sent me draws him."[157] It looks like peace not pressure!

"Do not go from house to house."

And to show us that this person of peace isn't a fluke, Jesus told them to settle into a long-term relationship with that person. It's not safe to go door to door. There really are too many wolves behind too many of the doors. So, Jesus will not only take you to a safe person, He will use that person to reach the others.

Many salesmen in America have sold products house to house. The more doors you knock on, the more product you will sell. This has often worked quite well in a free land with good products. But now people buy online or at stores. The days of peddling door to door are largely over. And, from the outset, NT Christianity was not to be peddled; but, to be shared by a faith that works through love. Paul said, *"For we are not like so many, peddlers of God's word...."*[158] We have been called to make disciples not consumers. We do not need to go house to house. God knows where those who hunger for truth and transformation, for salvation, live. And He will connect us with them, if we follow Jesus.

Pressuring people for a decision is very different from discipleship. Many have made quick prayers only to quickly depart from the Faith. Jesus did not advocate that approach to Kingdom building, nor do we. Read through the Gospels and Acts looking for the "people of peace" who were revealed by their openness and receptivity and then used by God to influence their whole town for Christ.

We go in peace, representing the Prince of Peace building the Kingdom of peace. *"For the kingdom of God is not a matter of eating and drinking but of righteousness and peace and joy in the Holy Spirit."*[159]Paul again pictures the disciple as a warrior who has, *"shod our feet with the*

---

157 John 6:44
158 2 Corinthians 2:17; Ephesians 4:15
159 Romans 14:17

preparation of the gospel of peace."[160] We have shoes of peace as part of the whole armor of God.

In many ways, it was these precious promises by our loving Savior that won the Pakistanis over to NT Discipleship. Fear could no longer cancel the call to *"go and make disciples."* Because our all-powerful Savior has promised to go with every disciple maker unto the end of the age. I could now give the believing disciples of Pakistan the same promise that Paul gave, even to Romans, who were living in the deadly presence of Emperor Nero: *"The God of peace will soon crush Satan under your feet."*[161] Hallelujah!

160 Ephesians 6:15 - NKJV
161 Romans 16:20

Chapter Eleven

Multiplication and Healing

"Whenever you enter a town and they receive you,
eat what is set before you." Luke 10:8-9

Sometimes, entire towns today are welcoming and receiving Christ's disciples. Good news travels fast. We should expect a great God of salvation to do a great work of salvation. Think of it. Jesus did not say, Go and disciple your neighbor. He said, *"make disciples of all nations."* Nations, entire people groups, or cultural communities, are to be won. If Jesus wants whole nations discipled, then He must have given a way for that very thing to be possible. And that, exactly, is what is happening today. Whole communities are being transformed. Mass movements are giving birth to new movements! The number of disciples worldwide is doubling every 3.5 years! [162] True Christianity is multiplying by the power of the Holy Spirit!

Picture the difference between adding converts and multiplying disciples.

Consider, one evangelist wins one convert every day over 10 years, That's 365 x10 = 3650 converts, often by pressurized, pray-this-prayer-after-me decisional evangelism. This would, no doubt, represent tremendous daily effort. But it would also demand an almost robotic focus and conversation manipulation, daily, to get the person to the place where they are willing to pray the prayer. Which of us has ever known someone to do this, at least for very long. It is not a reasonable, duplicable method of evangelism. The pressure involved in this way is enormous.

Consider, one disciple who wins one person of peace each year for 10 years with only 10, then, personally being won. But discipling never stops. Every new disciple also finds a person of peace and makes a disciple every year, also. Multiplication by peace without pressure through a very duplicable "each one reach one each

---

[162] See Miraculous Movements by Jerry Trousdale; The Father Glorified by Pat Robertson; and the Jan/Feb issue of Frontiers magazine for articles on DMMs, including both practical and data analyses

year method" of discipleship evangelism. The peacefulness involved in this way is unimaginable.

Year 1	1x2 = 2	Year 6	32x2 = 64
Year 2	2x2 = 4	Year 7	64x2 =128
Year 3	4x2 = 8	Year 8	126x2 = 256
Year 4	8x2 = 16	Year 9	256x2 = 512
Year 5	16x2 = 32	Year 10	512x2 = 1024

By year 15, converts won = 5,475
    Vs By year 15, disciples won = 32,768

By year 20, converts won = 7,300
    Vs By year 20, disciples won = 1,048,576

Imagine the growth if every Christian was a disciple who made one disciple a year! Today's DMMs, which are defined as 1000 new disciples won over 4/5 years by 4 streams of disciples, are showing incredible growth. But, if each disciple was a disciple maker, the growth would be even exponentially greater because even in DMMs not everyone reproduces! Let us pray for such a truly Contagious Disciple Making![163] You can see how whole regions could be quickly impacted.

One of the main methods of discipling that many Christ followers are using to disciple people of peace is called the Discovery Bible Study (DBS). It is a way of amazing peace without pressure. The DBS way of discipling is very easily mastered, as they are discovering in Pakistan! I only introduced it by explaining two bookmarks we had translated into Urdu. See Appendix Four for an introduction to DBS. Mastering the ability to facilitate a Discovery Bible Study with a person of peace is a major tool of many laborers whom God is placing into the harvest, today, across the world.

DBS is obedience driven and powerfully blessed by the Spirit of God. It will never leave a person as a hearer of the Word

---

[163] The name of David and Paul Watson's classic book on Discipleship and DMMs, written in 2014

only and not a doer.[164] But, rather, as James promised, one who is truly *"blessed in his doing."*[165] So many Christians are passive hearers. Disciples are receptive and responsive hearers, as Jesus promised, *"If you know these things, blessed are you if you do them."*[166]

"Whenever you enter a town and they receive you, eat what is set before you."

The command to eat everything that a person of peace sets before the discipler humbles the going disciple, lessening expectations and demands. It is also opening the door to the Gentile world and away from a strictly Jewish, kosher diet approach. This is one way that the sending of the 72 differed from the earlier sending of the 12. Then, Jesus first commanded them, *"Go nowhere among the Gentiles and enter no town of the Samaritans, but go rather to the lost sheep of the house of Israel."*[167] This restriction was lifted by Jesus for the Apostles and the whole Church when He gave them the Great Commission.

"Heal the sick in it"

I will never forget the day when a dear pastor friend and I were talking about DMMs and Luke 10. The moment his eyes read verse 9, he declared, "that's my problem with Luke 10 today." You see, Christ's including, *"Heal the sick,"* was a command he couldn't handle. I felt sorry for him. He was blocked from the blessings of NT Discipleship and DMMs by three words. His theology did not have the room to open up for the reality, power and blessings of Luke 10. Nothing that I could say could open his mind. This is an example of the parable Jesus told to the Pharisees when discussing the vast differences between their ways of discipleship.[168]

---

[164] See James 1:22-25
[165] James 1:25
[166] John 13:17
[167] Matthew 10:5-6; see also Acts 11:19-20 where there is obvious confusion about going beyond the early restriction and entering into the global harvest field
[168] See Luke 5:33-39

"He told them a parable: '...No one puts new wine into old wineskins. If he does, the new wine will burst the skins and it will be spilled, and the skins will be destroyed. But new wine must be put into fresh wineskins. And no one after drinking old wine desires new, for he says, 'The old is good.'"

My dear friend was satisfied with the old wine he had been taught and experienced. Only a miracle of grace by the revelation of the Holy Spirit can open such a one to the new wine of DMMs via Luke 10. Why? Because, sadly, for them, the old wine is perfectly fine.[169] They have no taste for something else. They are fatally stuck. That is why Jesus says, "No one...." It's impossible to teach someone what he thinks he already knows. How sad it is, but it is possible for someone who was once receptive to the miraculous, to lose their taste and belief in it.[170]

Why do I believe Luke 10 applies literally to today? I will write a few reasons, but the blessing I saw in Pakistan was that I did not have to prove that healing prayer is still operational. That it is a blessing given to every disciple, today! They already knew it. Do you believe it? So, why is healing prayer still for disciples of Christ?

1. Because there is nothing in Luke 10 that restricts the time only to that day.
2. Because their healing and deliverance work was in the name of Jesus (10:17), just like ours is, so it was not their inherent authority or power, but it was derived from and operated through Him.
3. Because this does not demand that every disciple have "the gift of healing," just the ability to pray healing prayers for certain people and for divine protection.

---

[169] Luke 5:39

[170] Isn't it a miracle whenever someone is born again? Yet many "born again Christians" get locked back into the natural world. They lose their taste for the supernatural power of God.

4. Because the only ones for whom prayer is made is for the "receptive," that is those who are people of peace in the pathway of discipleship. Note, that the healing follows the receptivity – "*if they receive you...heal the sick in it.*"
5. Because this is a reality TODAY, being done in answer to prayer by disciples all over the world following Luke 10, me included. Part of the training needed to work in the harvest is training in healing prayer, which the 72 had, and I have received and which I give as part of my Spirit Empowered Discipleship training sessions, time permitting.
6. Because in Pakistan we saw God heal, following the trainings, as we briefly prayed for those needing healing who either believed in healing, or were brought forward by others who did.
7. Because Jesus was "*anointed by God with the Holy Spirit and with power. And he went about doing good and healing all those who were oppressed by the devil, for God was with Him*"[171] – and we follow Jesus!
8. Because the OT is full of divine healing[172] and there is more grace, not less, under the New Covenant than under the old.
9. Because "*He took up our infirmities, and carried our sorrows... and by his wounds we are healed,*"[173] according to the faith God gives us in His Word.
10. Because the NT is full of divine healing, as well as the rest of the history of Christ's followers up to today, especially and in a more concentrated manner since the 20th Century's 3rd Great Awakening in the USA[174] and across the earth.

Your use of and success with healing prayer reveals much more than you may have been led to think. How can we think that we are the followers of the Jesus of the NT and be indifferent to His life-

---

[171] Acts 10:38

[172] See Exodus 15:26; 23:25; Deuteronomy 7:12-15, 32, 39, 47; 28:15-27, 59; 1 Samuel 5:6; 2 Kings 20:5; 2 Chronicles 7:13-14; Psalm 25; 30:2,5; 41:1-4; 103:3; 107:17-20; Jeremiah 30:12-17; Hosea 11:1-3;

[173] Isaiah 53:4-5; Matthew 8:17; 1 Peter 2:24-25

[174] I have never heard a cessationist refer to the Pentecostal/Charismatic revival of the 20th century as the 3rd Great Awakening, though it absolutely and unequivocally was just that. We ignored and denied it- against all evidence.

giving promises? To His constant and never-failing practice of healing? There is no account of anyone coming to Him needing healing or deliverance, whom He left sick or demonized![175] To a despised and destitute leper, who knelt before Him saying, "*Lord, if you will, you can make me clean,*" He replied, "*I will; be clean.*"[176] Yet millions of Christians in the USA say, "*I won't. That's impossible today,*" while affirming that true prayer in Jesus' name can do anything!

"and say to them, 'the kingdom of God has come near to you.'"

The kingdom of God is the rule and reign of Jesus Christ. Wherever He reigns, there is His kingdom. The devil is a usurping, dispossessed leader, with a large, evil, somewhat organized army. We who follow Jesus today, enjoy a union with Him even greater than the 72 had when they were sent out. Our benefits as disciples of the crucified and risen Lord are also greater than theirs were when He sent them out! Those born again by a living faith are literally united with Jesus in His crucifixion, death, resurrection and ascended glory.[177] "*Blessed be the God and Father of our Lord Jesus Christ, who has blessed us in Christ with every spiritual blessing in the heavenly places!*"[178] Wherever we go in His name, He goes. Our bodies are the temples of the Holy Spirit. We have been delivered from "*the domain of darkness and transferred into the kingdom of his beloved Son*"[179] The devil is a defeated foe who cannot touch us if we abide in Christ by a living faith. In fact, if we will submit ourselves to God and resist the devil, he must flee from us, so great is our victory in Christ! The victory and power of Christ are ours.[180] One of the reasons so few live in this victory is because it is the role of the Spirit of God to reveal to us what Christ has given to us. When He is resisted, grieved and quenched, so His benefits are hidden from us.

---

[175] See Matthew 4:23; 14:14; 15:30; Mark 3:10; 6:56; Luke 7:22; Acts 10:38
[176] Matthew 8:1-3
[177] Romans 6:5-11; Colossians 3:1-3
[178] Ephesians 1:3
[179] Colossians 1:13
[180] See James 4:7-8; I Peter 5:6-9; Romans 8:37

"Now we have received not the spirit of the world, but the Spirit who is from God, that we might understand the things freely given us by God."[181]

We must not underestimate who we are as the "children of God."[182] We are "heirs of God and fellow heirs with Christ,"[183] and meant "to reign in life through the one man, Jesus Christ."[184] Our union with Christ by faith is so powerful that Jesus reminded the 72, *"The one who hears you hears me, and the one who rejects you rejects me, and the one who rejects me rejects the one who sent me."*[185]

So, like the 72, wherever we go, we bring the glory and the power of the kingdom of God within us. It is near to everyone we draw near to, because Christ is in us and He is King of kings and Lord of lords. What a privilege to go into all the world in His name! Join us in believing, receiving, and going into all the world.

---

[181] 1 Corinthians 2:12 and see Psalm 103!
[182] 1 John 3:1; Romans 8:16
[183] Romans 8:17
[184] Romans 5:17
[185] Luke 10:16

Chapter Twelve

Rejection and Warning
Luke 10:10-12[186]

We are now near the end. And as I spoke through this final passage, my audiences in Pakistan sensed that I was truly not speaking for myself, but for Christ. For these are words of warning to all who reject the way of NT Discipleship and the disciples sent to them by the mercy of King Jesus, Himself. So, please *"take care how you hear, for to the one who has, more will be given, and from the one who has not, even what he thinks he has will be taken away."*[187] And now read prayerfully and slowly the final instructions given to the 72.

> *"But whenever you enter a town and they do not receive you, go into its streets and say, 'Even the dust of your town that clings to our feet we wipe off against you.' Nevertheless, know this, that the kingdom of God has come near. I tell you: it will be more bearable on that day for Sodom than for that town.'"*

These actions were not strange to the Jews who heard of them in Jesus' day. They were the actions that Pharisees would take when leaving a Gentile or "unclean" town. They saw it as an action of cursing. We see it as an action of warning. And I always, at this point am filled with a fervent spirit that pleads with my hearers not to reject the grace of God that has been shared with them, in Jesus' name. I prayerfully do so also to you, my readers.

It might surprise you to learn that many years after the 72 went out, the various missionary teams of Paul practiced this. More than once, on people with Jewish backgrounds who rejected the good news of the kingdom that they were sharing, they obeyed this

---

[186] Though the context continues further, I always had to stop here because this was all the time I had at each meeting. It always took 4-5 hours to get this far. You can read the rest of the story of Luke 10 in Appendix Five.
[187] Luke 8:18

command of Jesus.[188] If a people or town were resistant, then they were to move on. Just like the 12 and the 72, when they were earlier sent out. Unless the Spirit of God told them differently, as He did to Paul in Corinth when He assured him, *"Do not be afraid, but go on speaking and do not be silent, for I am with you, and no one will attack you to harm you, for I have many in this city who are my people."*

So, whether I am in Asia, America or Africa, I remind those to whom I speak,

> *"Do not be deceived: God is not mocked, for whatever one sows, that will he also reap... And let us not grow weary of doing good, for in due season we will reap, if we do not give up."*[189]

My prayer for all of you is that you will receive this message and not resist the Spirit and grace of God. Join us, with great faith, in seeing the mighty blessings of Christ flow into the nations more widely than ever before. For it is happening. DMMs are very real, and the USA is, largely, being left untouched by these great movements of the Spirit of God. Peter explained why some are left in a blinded state as He boldly bore witness to the Sanhedrim who, in their days, were resisting the movement of the same Spirit.

> *"And we are witnesses of these things, and so is the Holy Spirit, whom God has given to those who obey him."*[190]

So, if you live in Pakistan, America, Guatemala, Greece, South Africa or China – indeed, wherever you may live, follow Christ obediently like the first disciples did. Be filled with and led by the Holy Spirit. And you will be blessed as you are made a blessing wherever you go and are led to abide, even for an hour. And always, every day and everywhere, be blessed by keeping in mind the last Great Commission of our Lord Jesus,

---

[188] See Acts 13:44-52 and 18:5-11
[189] Galatians 6:7-9
[190] Acts 5:32

"All authority in heaven and on earth has been given to me. Therefore go and make disciples of all nations, baptizing them in the name of the Father and of the Son and of the Holy Spirit, and teaching them to obey everything I have commanded you. And surely I am with you always, to the very end of the age."[191]

---

[191] Matthew 28:18-20 (NIV)

Appendix One

Conclusions from my NT Discipleship Research

Here's a brief summary of some 20+ truths that I have learned:

- The word "Christian" is used only three times in the whole NT while the word "disciple" (disciples) is used 250+ times in the NT
- Jesus, every rabbi and NT era disciple following them, agreed what "disciple" meant and shared the same expectations of their disciples
- Jesus, following other rabbis, made disciples who were expected to build their "group" (house/family) by making other disciples
- So, when Jesus commanded, "make disciples of the nations," those who obeyed Him would clearly know whether they had fulfilled His Commission
- The four gospels have as one of their major goals, the defining, depicting and deployment of disciples, ie – their entire training
- Jesus followed 4 steps in making disciples: (1) Watch how I make you disciples (2) We will make other disciples together (3) I will watch you try to make disciples and give you interaction (4) Then you will be ready to go and make disciples who make disciples
- Jesus is both the King of the Kingdom of God (over all creation) and the Head of His Church (His Body of human followers)
- Jesus defeated Satan, sin and death by His crucifixion, resurrection and ascension – calling His followers into a faith-union with His victory, as they help advance His

Kingdom, build His Church and oppose Satan's strategies of deception and destruction in Jesus' name

- Jesus desired, taught, prayed for and gave His Spirit to achieve the unity of His followers
- Jesus demanded a commitment to prayer, in general, and to the Harvest Prayer, in particular, as the first step of His disciple making strategy
- Jesus clearly taught the first disciples that they needed to be filled with the Holy Spirit in order to fulfill His Commission, extend His Kingdom and build His Church
- The Holy Spirit can be resisted, grieved and quenched by sin in individuals or in church communities, resulting in a significant loss of spiritual power and blessing in extending Christ's Kingdom
- Paul was a disciple of Gamaliel who became a disciple of Jesus
- Paul's supreme strategy, once trained, was to make disciples wherever he went through his individual and mission team efforts
- The NT was written by disciples to disciples who were committed to making other disciples by the power of the Holy Spirit
- Jesus promised to be present with all disciples who lived to fulfill His Great Commission until the present age ends with His Second Coming
- The Early Church was more-or-less committed to this task for the first 300 years of its existence
- From Constantine to the Reformation, the Church went through declines and revivals marking decades of either darkness or growth
- Every revival, reformation or renewal was basically a recommitment to NT Discipleship, ie a return to following Jesus by the power of the Spirit crossing denominational borders and affecting lost souls and the present culture

- The 21st century is an unparalleled time of the renewal of NT Discipleship resulting in faster discipleship multiplication and church planting in Christ's Kingdom than any period since the Book of Acts
- It has been the devil's strategy from the Ascension of Jesus, to divert the disciples' attention from fulfilling Christ's Great Commission in Christ's ordained way.
- Since the Word of God contains the words and teachings of Jesus, the devil attempts to distract disciples from carefully studying and faithfully following the teachings of the living Word of God. He supports strategies that oppose Jesus' clear teaching and example. And Satan ever tempts the disciple with sin.

Some of the Commands of Jesus

<u>35 Commands of Jesus in "The Sermon on the Mount"</u>

<u>No.</u>	<u>Text</u>	<u>Command</u>
1.	5:12	Rejoice and be glad (when personally opposed)
2.	5:16	Let your light shine before others
3.	5:17	Do not even imagine that Jesus opposes the Law
4.	5:23-24	Leave (worship) go and be reconciled to offended brother
5.	5:25-26	Settle serious problems with others quickly
6.	5:29-30	Deal seriously with whatever leads you to sin
7.	5:34	Do NOT swear or depend on establishing your veracity by invoking God in an oath
8.	5:37	Think carefully before peaking and always tell the simple truth. Be true to your word
9.	5:38	Do NOT take the law into your own hands
10.	5:39-41	Endure loss for the Kingdom by allowing personal insult (turn the other cheek for a slap), property loss (cloak), and forced service (going extra mile) rather than grasping on to worldly ways and personal rights and privileges.
11.	5:42	Give to the one asking and loan generously
12.	5:44	Love your enemies
13.	5:44	Pray for your opponents and persecutors

14.	5:48	Be perfected by love—by God filling you
15.	6:1	Do NOT serve to be seen by others
16.	6:2	Do NOT draw attention to yourself when giving to the needy
17.	6:3	Be secretive and behind-the-scenes in helping others in need
18.	6:5	Do NOT pray insincerely, to be seen or heard
19.	6:6	Pray in secret
20.	6:7	Do NOT pray using thoughtless, repetitive words
21.	6:9-13	Use "The Lord's Prayer" as a model for prayer
22.	6:16	Do NOT fast to impress others with your sacrifice
23.	6:17	Fast only in God's sight, not in others'
24.	6:19	Do NOT make any earthly thing your treasure
25.	6:20, 24	Set your heart on eternity and work for God
26.	6:25,31,34	Do NOT worry (about your physical life or future)
27.	6:33	Seek to advance God's Kingdom and glory FIRST –all the time and in everything
28.	7:1	Do NOT judge other's motives or condemn them
29.	7:5	Deal with your own sin FIRST (repent in faith)
30.	7:6	Do be discerning and do NOT waste time on mockers
31.	7:7	Seek God's help through persistent prayer
32.	7:12	Always do to others exactly what you want done to you

33.	7:13,21	Enter God's Kingdom through the narrow gate of the Living and written Word of God
34.	7:15	Beware and stay away from false teachers (whose lives betray their words)
35.	7:24-27	Hear and OBEY (practice) the words of Christ

General Commands of Jesus – in Mark's Gospel

1. "Repent and believe the good news!" (1:15)
2. "Come, follow me and I will make you fishers of men." (1:17)
3. "He who has ears to hear, let him hear." (4:18)
4. "Consider carefully what you hear." (concerning Christ's teaching (4:24)
5. "Go in peace" (5:34)
6. "Don't be afraid. Just believe." (5:36)
7. "Take courage. Don't be afraid." (6:48)
8. "If anyone would come after me, he MUST deny himself and take up his cross and follow me." (8:34)
9. "Do not stop him…for whoever is not against us is for us." (9:39)
10. "Have salt among yourselves and be at peace with each other." (9:50)
11. "What God has joined together, let man not separate." (10:6)
12. "Let the little children come to me, and do not hinder them." (10:14)
13. "Not so with you. Instead, whoever wants to be great among you must be your servant, and whoever wants to be first must be slave to all." (10:43-44)
14. "Have faith in God." (11:22)
15. "Therefore, I tell you, whatever you ask for in prayer, believe that you have received it, and it will be yours." (11:24)
16. "And when you stand praying, if you hold anything against anyone, forgive him, so that your Father in heaven may forgive your sins." (11:25)

17. "Love the Lord your God with all your heart and with all your soul and with all your mind and with all your strength. The second is this: Love your neighbor as yourself." (12:30-31)
18. "And the gospel must be preached to all nations." (Mark 13:10)
19. "Be on guard! Be alert!" (13:33)
20. "Therefore, keep watch because you do not know when the owner of the house will come back…. If he comes suddenly do not let him find you sleeping. What I say to you, I say to everyone, Watch!" (13:35-37)
21. "Take it, this is my body. Then he took the cup, gave thanks and offered it to them, and they all drank from it." (14:22-23)
22. "Watch and pray so that you will not fall into temptation. The spirit is willing, but the body is weak." (14:38)
23. "Go into all the world and preach the gospel to all creation." (16:15)

Appendix Three

A Summary of The Person and Work of the Holy Spirit

Names/Ministries of the Spirit in this Age*

1. The Divine Tenant (Rom 8:9)
2. Paraclete-Comforter/Encourager (Jn 14:16;Acts 9:31)
3. The Spirit of Truth (Jn 14:17)
4. The Teacher (Jn 14:26)
5. The Remembrancer (Jn 14:26)
6. The Center of the Assembly (Acts 15:28)
7. The Witness/Vicar of Christ (Jn 15:26)
8. The Communicator/Echo of Christ (Jn 16:13-14)
9. The Successor of Christ (Jn 7:39)
10. The Advocate/Intercessor (Rom 8:26)
11. The Helper (Jn 14:26)
12. The Conveyor of His Glory (Jn 16:15; Eph 3:16-17)
13. The Spirit of Holiness (Rom 1:4)
14. The Guide/Leader (Jn 16:13; Rom 8:14)
15. The Anointing (of Christ)-1 Jn 2:20, 27
16. The Sanctifier (Rom 15:16; 1 Thes 5:23)
17. The Joy-Giver (Rom 14:17;1 Thess 1:6)
18. The Commander (Acts 1:2)
19. The Spirit of the Lord (Isa 11:2;Isa 61:1)
20. The Power of the Highest (Lk 1:35)
21. Spirit of Wisdom (Isa 11:2; Eph 1:17)
22. The Spirit of Revelation/Revelator (Eph 1:17)
23. The Spirit of knowledge (Isa 11:2…)
24. The Spirit of the fear of the Lord (Isa 11:2; Mtt10:28)
25. The Regenerator (John 3:5; Titus 3:5)
26. The Spirit of renewal (Titus 3:5; Acts 3:20)
27. The Sealer (Eph 1:13; 4:30)
28. The Guarantee/Down Payment (Eph 1:14)
29. The Promise (Lk 24:49; Acts 2:38)
30. The Believers' Filler (Acts 4:8, 31; 6:5; Eph 5:18)

31. The Author of Scripture (2 Sam 23:2,3; Mk 12:36; Acts 1:16; Heb 3:7; 2 Pet 1:21)
32. The Keeper/Preserver (1 Thess 5:23)
33. The 9 Fruit Producer (Gal. 5:22-23)
34. The Partner/Communer (2 Cor 13:14)
35. The Lifegiver (John 6:63; Rom 8:2)
36. The Executor of the Redemption of the Cross of Christ (Rom 8:13)
37. The Lord (2 Cor 3:18)
38. The Liberator (2 Cor 3:17)
39. The Spirit of Glory (1 Pet 4:14)
40. The Spiritual Giftgiver (1 Cor 12:4-11)
41. The Inviter (Rev 22:17)
42. The Ordainer of God's servants (Acts 20:28)
43. The Withdrawer (1 Thes 5:19)
44. The Breath of God (John 20:22; Job 27:3)
45. The Preacher (1 Pet 1:12)
46. The Instiller of God's Will (Rom 8:26-27)
47. The Uniter (Eph 4:3-4)
48. The Conductor of Worship (1 Cor 12,14)
49. The Empowerer (Eph 3:16)
50. The Executor of the Great Commission (Acts 1:8)
51. The Convicter (John 16:8)
52. The Caller of missionaries (Acts 13:2)
53. The Propeller into the work (Acts 13:4)
54. The Sustainer thru suffering (Acts 13:52; 1 Thes 1:6)
55. The Problem Solver (Acts 15:28)
56. The Forbidder (Acts 16:6,7)
57. The Still Small Voice (Rom 8:16; Gal 5:25; Rev 2:7)
58. The Evangel of Grace (2 Cor 3:3,6)
59. The Author of Conscience (Rom 9:1)
60. The Spirit of Supplication (Zech 12:10; Rom 8:15)

*The Names were given or derived from studying AJ Gordon's "The Ministry of the Spirit" (1894)

Appendix Four

Introduction to Discovery Bible Study - DBS

The discovering of the DBS method of discipling through Bible stories was an amazing revelation given to missionaries earnestly beseeching the Father for the best way to make disciples and fulfill the Great Commission. It's major biblically-grounded elements are these 10 characteristics:

1. God is the Teacher not man because we do not need to be taught by man
2. Everyone taught by God will come to salvation through Jesus
3. Prayer is more important, more basic for the discipler than is anything else
4. People learn more through personal discovery than through lecture
5. God expects those He teaches to do something with what they learn
6. If they obey the conviction of the Holy Spirit, God will draw closer to them
7. This process leads to having faith in Jesus as God's only way of salvation
8. Those taught should share with other receptive people of peace
9. The DNA of a true church should be sown into the DBS group
10. As disciples are made and baptized, churches will be planted and multiply

Since during the NT era many could not read, making disciples does not depend on literacy. Disciples can be made and simple churches established by story and truth telling even among the illiterate.

Rabbis taught mainly by questioning rather than by lecturing. They had the wisdom of knowing where a disciple needed to develop and asked questions to help him move forward. Jesus followed this method, too.

So, read and reflect on the following Scriptures to understand that DBS has a solid, biblical basis:

- John 6:44-45
- 1 John 2:20, 27
- Hebrews 5:11-14
- Romans 15:14 with 12:7
- Matthew 7:21-23 with James 1:22-25

Now we offer to you the same info on bookmarks that disciples are using globally

1. 1A – Luke 10:1-11
2. 1B – DMM Prayer
3. 2A – Person of peace questions and 28 biblical stories
4. 2B – DBS questions guiding the discipling facilitator and partner

1A   ## 1B

LUKE 10:1-11

After this the Lord appointed seventy-two others and sent them on ahead of him, two by two, into every town and place where he himself was about to go.

And he said to them, "The harvest is plentiful, but the laborers are few. Therefore pray earnestly to the Lord of the harvest to send out laborers into his harvest.

Go your way; behold, I am sending you out as lambs in the midst of wolves.

Carry no moneybag, no knapsack, no sandals, and greet no one on the road.

Whatever house you enter, first say, 'Peace be to this house!'

And if a son of peace is there, your peace will rest upon him. But if not, it will return to you.

And remain in the same house, eating and drinking what they provide, for the laborer deserves his wages. Do not go from house to house.

Whenever you enter a town and they receive you, eat what is set before you.

Heal the sick in it and say to them, 'The kingdom of God has come near to you.'

But whenever you enter a town and they do not receive you, go into its streets and say,

Even the dust of your town that clings to our feet we wipe off against you. Nevertheless know this, that the kingdom of God has come near.'

DMM PRAYER TIME

Welcome to this prayer time! Our LORD and Master Jesus Christ has gathered us together in this place. We will pray together for the Holy Spirit to come upon us with great power and conviction, leading to a Disciple Making Movement (DMM). Jesus said to His disciples: *If you abide in me, and my words abide in you, ask whatever you wish, and it will be done for you.* John 15:7

Let us remain in Him, make out desires His and seek His blessing.

DMM PRAYER GUIDE

More workers for the harvest.
Luke 10:2 *And he said to them, "The harvest is plentiful, but the laborers are few. Therefore pray earnestly to the Lord of the harvest to send out laborers into his harvest.*

Finding People of Peace
Luke 10:5-6 *Whatever house you enter, first say, 'Peace be to this house!' And if a son of peace is there, your peace will rest upon him. But if not, it will return to you.*

For multiplication of disciples.
Matthew 13:8 *Other seeds fell on good soil and produced grain, some a hundredfold, some sixty, some thirty.*

Against spiritual warfare.
Ephesians 6:11 *Put on the whole armor of God, that you may be able to stand against the schemes of the devil.*

2A   2B

Would you like to discover for yourself what God is like and how God wants you to live? Who could you invite to discover God with you?

VERSES TO STUDY

Genesis 1:1-25
Genesis 2:4-24
Genesis 3:1-13
Genesis 3:14-24
Genesis 6:5-8
Genesis 6:9-8:14
Genesis 12:1-8, 15:1-6, 17:1-7

Genesis 22:1-19
Exodus 12:1-28
Exodus 20:1-21
Leviticus 4:1-35
Isaiah 53
Luke 1:26-38; 2:1-20

Matthew 3; John 1:29-31
Matthew 4:1:11
John 3:1-21
John 4:1-26, 39-42
Luke 5:17-26
Mark 4:35-41
Mark 5:1-20

John 11:1-44
Matthew 26:17-30
John 18:1-19:16
Luke 23:32-56
Luke 24:1-35
Luke 24:36-53
John 3:1-21

Illustration © 2009 by Brian W. Chalmers.
Used by permission.
This image and more on Brian Chalmers's
website at www.Brisbiblestories.com

DISCOVERY
BIBLE
STUDY
QUESTIONS

Part 1

1. Ask: What are you thankful for this week?

2. Ask: What are you struggling with and how can we help?

3. Ask: Did you do the "I will" statement you made last week? What happened as a result of your obedience?

4. Ask: With whom did you share last week's story with and how did it go?

Part 2

1. Ask: God is teaching us in this week's passage.

2. Ask: someone to read the passage.

3. Ask: someone to read the passage again.

4. Ask: for someone to retell the passage in his own words as if to someone who wasn't there.

5. Ask: Did they add or leave out anything when they retold the story? If something is missed that isn't there, ask, "Where did you find that in the passage?" Must focus only on what is in the passage.

6. Ask: What does this passage teach us about God?

7. Ask: What does this passage teach us about mankind?

8. Ask: If we believe this passage is from God, what behavior must we change this week?

9. Ask: Who are you going to share this passage with this week?

10. Ask: When do you want to meet again?

Final words

- Start the 1st DBS study with Part 2
- Do not allow any importing of answers from outside the story
- Do not teach or give answers or "steer" the discussion – let the Spirit lead
- Have your 2x2 partner write down all answers to 6-8
- You also do an "I will statement" each week and report as per Part 1, Q3
- Encourage everyone to share the story with someone receptive during week
- Expect God to mightily move, even miraculously
- Do Part 1 in all subsequent DBS group meetings
- Recognize that Qs 1-4 are planting the DNA of a true church in the group
- PRAY, PRAY, PRAY
- Ask the Lord if this group should become a church plant or join an already established receptive church (group)
- Always be available for counsel with your disciples
- Pray for 4 leading disciples who will make 4 other disciples over 4 years, leading to a DMM
- Have extensive seasons of prayer and fasting together with other disciples
- Get aware of what is happening in DMMs globally via justinlong.org

Appendix Five

The Rest of the Luke 10 Account

Luke 10:13-16 - Reassurances by Jesus

The parallel text of this passage is found in Matthew 11:21-24. In that place Jesus is denouncing *"the cities where most of his mighty works had been done, because they did not repent."* So, its place following the sending out of the 72 does not mean that it has any direct reference to their mission.

The relevant verse in Luke's passage states,

> **"The one who hears you hears me; and the one who rejects you rejects me. And the one who rejects me rejects the one who sent me."**

Here Jesus is reassuring the 72 and all whom He sends out on mission, that He takes personally how they are received and treated. That is encouraging because all too often those who hear us do not connect us with Jesus. It is vital that we see ourselves this way as that will certainly reinforce our need to pay close attention to our conduct and speech. If we sin, then we are not representing Jesus. But if we are guided by the Spirit, waiting on His promptings and direction, then we have the awesome reality of actually becoming the mouthpiece and representative of Jesus.

This fact, if grasped by faith, encourages every disciple on mission anywhere with the presence of Jesus. Paul captured this reassuring reality when he affirmed,

> *"But thanks be to God, who in Christ always leads us in triumphal procession, and through us spreads the fragrance of the knowledge of him everywhere. For we are the aroma of Christ to God among those who are being saved and among those who are perishing, to one a*

fragrance from death to death, to the other a fragrance of life to life. Who is sufficient for these things?"[192]

Luke 10:17-20   Return and Debriefing

This passage is filled with special revelation concerning the mission of the 72 and the mission we are on today as disciples in the harvest.

"*The seventy-two returned with joy, saying, 'Lord, even the demons are subject to us in your name!'*"

First, note that they all returned with joy, not some of them. Theirs was a mission of total victory, unmixed with stress and failure. How exceptional this is when we consider that they were all sent out "as lambs in the midst of wolves." So what was the score? Lambs 72 -Wolves 0! What an encouragement for all those disciples wanting to fulfill the Great Commission in contexts of opposition!

Second, observe that their whole success lay in their ministering "in the name of Jesus!" Now, we would not have known that had they not reported it here. In fact, looking just at the words of Jesus in 10:1-12, we might mistakenly think that the 72 were granted special, unique authority. They were not! Like us, their whole success depended on ministering in the name of Jesus.

What does it mean for us that, *"whatever you do in word and deed to do everything in the name of the Lord Jesus?"*[193] It is just this, to be absolutely convinced by faith that the risen and reigning Jesus is standing with us, ready to support us in everything we say or do for His glory and in accordance with His Word and Spirit. It is this truth that has ever empowered God's children to live and minister with such power and fruitfulness.

I cannot accurately relate what strength I have found in recently reading the astonishing biographies of people like George Muller, AJ Gordon, AB Simpson, John G Lake, Evan Roberts, Rees Howells, William Seymour, Watchman Nee, Smith Wigglesworth,

---

[192] C Corinthians 2:14-16
[193] Colossians 3:16

Martyn Lloyd Jones, Lester Sumrall, and Brother Yun (the Heavenly man). There is no possible way to describe their faith and life other than these men were usually serving God and mankind in the power of Jesus, many of them, literally fulfilling Christ's promise, *"Truly, truly, I say to you, whoever believes in me will also do the works that I do; and greater works than these will he do, because I am going to the Father."*[194] I doubt that anyone could read even a few of these biographies, and the messages of these men, without believing in the importance of experiencing a post-conversion baptism with and daily empowering of the Holy Spirit.

> *"I saw Satan fall like lightning from heaven. Behold, I have given you authority to tread on serpents and scorpions, and over all the power of the enemy, and nothing shall hurt you. Nevertheless, do not rejoice in this that the spirits are subject to you, but rejoice that your names are written in heaven."*

The 72 were living and ministering with miraculous evidences of the presence of Christ in much that they did. There is nothing in the entire NT that would make us believe that such should not accompany all His disciples until He returns. The fact that so few see the Christ-exalting power of God in their lives and work is our blame not His. Mark's gospel closes with what was the norm of NT disciples' living.[195] The resurgence of miracles through today's DMMs gives us evidence that the tide of the Spirit is rising and that revival is at hand, at least in those lands where repentance and faith return to NT era levels.

---

[194] John 14:12
[195] See Mark 16:14-20; Acts 1-28; Romans 1:11-12; 15:14-19; 1 Corinthians 2:1-5; 5:4-5; 12-14; 2 Corinthians 12:12-13; Galatians 3:1-6; Ephesians 1:3, 13-14, 15-23; 3:14-20; 6:10-20; 1 Thessalonians 1:4-10; 5:23; 2 Thessalonians 2:7-12; 2 Timothy 3:5; Hebrews 2:1-4; James 4:7-8; 5:13-18; 1 Peter 4:8-11; 5:6-11; 1 John 4:1-6; 5:18-19; Jude 8-9; Revelation 2:9, 13; 12:1-17; 13:7; 16:13-15; 20:4-6

Luke 10:21-24   Praise and Blessing

Suffice it for me to simply record the words spoken by Jesus in lieu of the victorious return and testimonies of the 72! May these words fill us with praise, knowing how blessed we are in virtue of our union with the heavenly-seated Christ and in the fact of our being the recipients of the gift of the Holy Spirit!

"In that same hour he rejoiced in the Holy Spirit and said, 'I thank you , Father, Lord of heaven and earth, that you have hidden these things from the wise and understanding and revealed them to little children; yes, Father, for such was your gracious will. All things have been handed over to me by my Father, and no one knows who the Son is except the Father, or who the Father is except the Son and anyone to whom the Son chooses to reveal him.' Then turning to the disciples, he said privately, 'Blessed are the eyes that see what you see! For I tell you that many prophets and kings desired to see what you see, and did not see it, and to hear what you hear, and did not hear it.'"

I welcome your response at ed.gross@comcast.net or at www.disciplesgo.com